THE
GOOD
BOOK
ON BUSINESS

Lessons from the wisest business teacher of all time

Second edition

DAVE KAHLE

The Good Book on Business

Lessons from the #1 bestseller of all time
Second Edition

Dave Kahle

This book is designed to provide accurate and authoritative information about the subject matter covered. This information is given with the understanding that neither the author nor The DaCo Corporation is engaged in rendering legal, professional advice. Since the details of your situation are fact dependent, you should additionally seek the services of a competent professional.

Published by The DaCo Corporation P.O. Box 523; Comstock Park, MI 49321 1.616.451.9377 | www.thegoodbookonbusiness.com Published in the United States of America

ISBN: 9781719840095; 0-9890008-8-5; 978-0-9899998-8-8

1. Religion

2. Business & Economics

CONTENTS

Why this book?

ONE

Why this book?

═══════════════════════════════

"I can't imagine how people can do what it takes to build a business without having a vision of a greater purpose for the business. It takes so much time, effort, and emotional energy. The saddest thing in the world is for some very successful business guy to look back on his efforts and say, 'So what?'"

Those are the comments from a CEO I interviewed in preparation for this book. His issue is at the heart of this book and lays the foundation for the objective of it as well. My purpose is to help you to see that your efforts are part of a bigger purpose, a higher calling, that will provide energy and direction and fulfillment in your career and your business.

We lead such incredibly busy lives these days. From the moment we awaken until we drop onto the pillow at night, we bounce from one "thing to do" to another in a frenzy of activity—e-mails, text messages, phone calls, people to see, and things to do.

Richard Swenson put it well in his book *Margin*:

The spontaneous tendency of our culture is to inexorably add detail to our lives: one more option, one more problem, one more commitment, one more expectation, one more purchase, one more debt, one more change, one more job, one more decision. We must now deal with more 'things per person' than at any other time in history.

That, by itself, is not necessarily a bad thing. I'm a type A personality, for example, and I thrive on having too much to do. It energizes me and brings out the best in me. I'm sure many of you experience the same kind of energy and exhilaration from the frenzy.

It's okay to be busy with a lot of things—as long as those things are the right things. And therein lies the issue. What if they are not? What if, at the end of your career, you look back with a certain degree of pride— you took this idea and brought it into fruition; you created an organization; you helped enrich a certain number of folks and provided a living for others. In so doing, you enjoyed the prosperity that accrued to you. Luxurious hotels, big homes, great vacations, the best of things—success!

And what if, after all of that, you asked yourself the question, "So what?" and had no answer?

What if, in those occasions in the stillness of the night, when you wake up and stare at the ceiling, or in the quiet of your office, before or after the crush of activity descends on you, where you have an opportunity to take a deep breath, to pause and reflect— you form the question, "Why? Why am I doing this?"

And what if you had no good answer?

Lack of purpose in life or business has been shown to increase a growing number of negative consequences. Increased use of drugs, alcohol abuse, depression, and thoughts of suicide grow in individuals who have no sense of purpose in their lives. Those that do have a strong sense of purpose live longer and are less likely to have heart disease and strokes.[1]

Again, the statistics don't matter in the middle of the night, when it is you who is lying awake, thinking about the meaning of all the time and effort you put into your business. Is the acquisition of more material goods the only reason why you do this? When is the house big enough, the car expensive enough, the trips lavish enough?

Why do you work so hard? What if you could discover a purpose for your business and your life that was bigger than anything you can conceive on your own? What if there were a purpose that reached down through generations and extended beyond what you can see now?

If you have ever questioned your purpose, if you have ever pondered a bigger purpose and a higher calling for your business, your career, and your life, then this book is for you. Biblical family businesses provide such a purpose.

Work-Life Integration

There is not a businessperson alive who doesn't struggle with balancing the demands of the job or business with the needs of his/her family. We live in a cloud of guilt. We could spend twenty hours a day at work, and whenever we leave, we leave things undone that could have been done. So we feel guilty about that. On the other hand, we could spend just as much time with our families. It seems like the time we devote to the job robs time from our families. Sometimes, we feel guilty just going to work.

The problem of work-family balance is becoming more acute every year. The Council of Economic Advisors reported that fathers reporting work-life conflict increased from 35 percent in 1977 to 60 percent in 2008.[2] That's almost double in less than one generation.

Of course, the problem for small business owners is even more acute. A survey by The Alternative Board found that half of all US business owners work more than fifty hours a week, and 20 percent work sixty or more hours.[3]

But regardless of the statistics, if you are a small business owner or operator, you know intimately the prevailing sense of guilt that seems to engulf you like a cloud wherever you are. Spend a little extra time at the business, and you feel guilty for not being with the family. Spend time with the family, and you can't help but feel guilty for what is not getting done at the business. It feels like a no-win situation.

Some even go so far as to give up on the idea. Sheryl Sandberg, COO of Facebook and author of the popular book *Lean In*, has argued, "There's no such thing as work-life balance. There's work, and there's life, and there's no balance."[4]

If only there were a way to more peacefully, rationally, and guiltlessly integrate work with our lives. What if there were a solution? What if there were a radical, outside-the-box solution that had been proven for countless generations and thousands of years? Biblical family businesses provide such a solution.

But there is more. Regardless of the potential impact on you, your business, and your family, the ideas in this book can impact the economy and our society should they be implemented in quantity and quality.

Almost everyone acknowledges that the current state of government indebtedness is unsustainable. Something in the economy has to change. This book offers one possible solution.

Stick with me, and you'll discover age-old solutions to many of our modern problems – solutions that have been ignored for generations. We'll discover what the Bible has to say about business. Before we do, let's deal with some common questions.

Why should I care what the Bible has to say about businesses?
Let's assume that you care about business or you would
not be reading this. Most folks who care about
business—be they entrepreneurs, would-be
entrepreneurs, businesspeople of all stripes, and those
who teach and mentor business people— want to do
better. It is just built into our DNA to strive for "more."

We all believe, at a deep, core level, that there is
more potential to our businesses and our careers than
what we see immediately in front of us. And we're
striving to attempt to reach that potential. This
incessant urge prods us to strive to be more, impact
more, influence more, make more, employ more, etc. It's
not just about making more money, although it is about
that. It is, more fundamentally, about achieving the
potential we suspect we have in ourselves and our
businesses. This urge for "more" provides the motivation
for the folks like us who buy the thousands of business
books written every year, attend the seminars, listen to
the podcasts, and watch the videos—all in an attempt
to learn something that will help make a positive
change in ourselves and our businesses.

We ascribe some credibility to the authors and
consultants whose ideas we seek. They are typically
individual consultants or teams of them who have
studied some segment of business or business behavior
and make some recommendations for our actions.

But what if we could go to the most unique book in the world, a collection of the best writing by forty-four authors, written over a span of 1,500 years and yet all shedding light on aspects of the same themes? What if we could dig out of that book a consistent set of guidelines, mindsets, and principles that would inform our quest to be more and achieve more? Wouldn't that be credibility and information of a higher level?

Thats why you should care. The information comes from a higher source.

Do I have to believe in the Bible and God to learn from this book?

No. There are a number of positions that people hold with regard to their opinion of the Bible. You can hold almost any of them and still gain from this book.

Think of these various positions as positions spread out on a continuum. At the end of the spectrum is the position "The Bible is word-for-word true and is the inspired Word of God, who authored it through the minds and hearts of the human writers." If that's your position, then clearly you will learn from this book.

Further down the spectrum are those who hold "The Bible is God's Word but can't be believed the word for word. It's more about concepts than details." If that's your position, you'll find the concepts we uncover in this manuscript to be extremely useful, even life-changing.

Further down the spectrum are those who hold "I'm

not sure the Bible is God's Word, but it clearly is a unique work and holds lots of wisdom that can help guide us." If that's where you are at, you'll find the wisdom that we uncover in this manuscript to be personal, practical, and assessable to the degree that it can change your businesses, your career, and maybe even the economy. As a practical matter, you may want to temporarily suspend your position about it being God's Word, as I often refer to it as such. It just makes it easier to see the connections between ideas expressed by writers who are generations apart. You can return to your beliefs after you have finished this book.

Further down the spectrum are those who hold this: "I don't know what I believe about the Bible. Millions of people seem to think it is special, but I haven't made up my mind." Fair enough. Let's leave that question in abeyance until you have finished this book. You may have some additional information to inform your opinion. Regardless, the ideas conveyed in the Bible stand on their own. Take them for what they are.

Finally, you may hold the position *"The Bible is a bunch of fables. I don't believe any of it."* You may not want to read any further. While the ideas, as I stated above, stand on their own, you need to have at least a little respect for the source of those ideas.

Is there a "Ten Commandments for businesspeople?"

Not exactly. There are some pretty specific commands

given to the Hebrews way back when that provide some excellent guidelines for us today.

Most of this book is focused on the picture that we can gain of a biblical business not by direct command but rather by seeing them in operation. While there are no "Thou shalt create a business" commands in the Bible, there are snapshots of dozens of businesses. As we look at each of these snapshots, we can put together a picture of what constitutes a biblical business. We learn about biblical businesses by seeing them in operation.

Are you advocating some religion?

Not a bit. This is about business, not religion. I think religion is one of the greatest evils perpetrated on humanity. But let's make sure we are using the same terms. There is a difference between religion and spirituality. Religion is characterized by buildings, rules, hierarchies, professionals, and institutions. Spirituality is about one's relationship with God. The two don't necessarily overlap.

When it comes to religions, I'm against them. When it comes to spirituality, I am a committed disciple of Jesus Christ.

Okay, now that I know where you stand, is there a difference between a nonbiblical and a biblical business?

Let me share with you the biblical business model, and you decide.

Hasn't Christianity in general advocated for biblical businesses?

Honestly, hardly at all. Business, specifically a biblically oriented business, has been terribly and almost universally misunderstood by the religious world.

The religious world has long looked at businesses as a necessary evil. Somebody has to make money to support their institutions, and so the religious institutions have tolerated businesses among their supporters, all the while holding that ministry, real ministry, is always done within the purview of the institutional church, or so the belief goes. What businesspeople do from Monday to Friday, therefore, has nothing to do with their standing in the institutional church scheme of things. This view of business has long been accepted without question by the movers and shakers in the religious establishment. It has been preached from the pulpit and acted on in countless ways.

That is slowly changing. Around the turn of the century, a movement known as "business as mission" (BAM) rose up and achieved some traction among both the institutional church adherents and a slice of the business community. The idea is that business—or at least an entity that calls itself a business—can penetrate certain geographies and people groups that are off limits to the institutional church. So the original advocates of BAM were motivated by traditional religious values. It wasn't that business had potential to be a powerful force for the Kingdom; it was that the business structure could be co-opted by the institutional church. So for them, a business was really a stealth arm of the institutional church.

In recent years, that idea has broadened a bit to allow that some businesses could have altruistic purposes beyond just making money. For example, a business supplying water wells to rural African villages would be accepted within the broad definitions of BAM, whereas a business that sold stocks to institutional investors would not.

Folks who advocate for this approach almost always come out of an institutional church background. Their focus is on the product sold by the business, and they often miss the processes and the relationships that are an integral part of any business.

While these concepts are encouraging and are a movement in the right direction, they miss the mark. The biblical view of business is not 'business as mission' (BAM), it is 'business is ministry' (BIM).

I am not naive enough to believe that this book alone is going to convince multitudes of people to change some of the paradigms that have been drilled into them by the church and the culture. The paradigms are too deeply embedded to be easily jettisoned.

But I believe I have a responsibility to add to the conversation. While the resistance to what I have to say may be extraordinary, my hope is that my saying it will release others to push forward. God has started a movement. We can jump into it and help touch people, improve people's lives, and change the world.

This book is divided into two sections. The first explores the biblical teaching on businesses, arriving at a conclusion that there is no other entity in the Kingdom of God that has more power and potential than a biblical business.

The second part addresses the questions that necessarily follow. If we actually accepted this idea and worked diligently to create a culture that encouraged and celebrated biblical business, what would be the implications? How would our economy be different? How would our families be different? What hinders us now? How could we go forward?

> God created work—and by extension, business— as the venue in which God would speak with man, relate to man, and work with man.

My premise is that if biblical businesses were embraced as God's primary means of penetrating the world with his Kingdom, and if only a fraction of the people who already have positions of influence were to promote the concept, we could transform the world.

And for the individual reader, here is the ultimate question: "What should I do?" Wherever you are at in your belief system or place in life, I am going to ask you to suspend your deep-seated paradigms of what a business is and consider some passages of Scripture in ways that you have probably never seen before. At the end of this book, if you see the vision for what a biblical business could and should be, you will experience a sense of freedom that you may never have experienced before. You will realize a sense of exhilaration and excitement at the possibilities that lie in front of you. In addition, you will have a renewed appreciation for the wisdom of God and the complexities and depth of his Kingdom.

TWO

In the Beginning

It is the early moments of creation. God is busy at work, creating the universe, and has just created his most complex entity: Man. Or, more specifically, the man Adam. He is a special creature, made in the image and likeness of God himself and placed at the very top of the created world.

How will God relate to Adam and his progeny? Will he create some special organization, like a church, and command Adam to worship him? Will he give Adam a family and expect that in the myriad decisions of raising children and getting along with his spouse Adam will seek him out for wisdom and guidance and thereby seek a relationship with God? What will God do with Adam? For what purpose did God create him?

He will give Adam a job. First, a lifetime purpose and then a specific task that contributes to that purpose. Then within the context of that job, God will work with Adam, speak to him, relate to him, and work together with him.

In other words, God created work—and by extension, business—as the venue in which God would speak with man, relate to man, and work with man.

Let us take a look:

> The Lord God took the man and put him in the Garden of Eden to work it and take care of it. (Gen. 2:15)

Here is Adam's life purpose: to work the Garden of Eden and take care of it. While the charge is specifically given to Adam, he was the first of the human race and set a precedent for the generations that were to come. In God's great plan, working and taking care of creation—not just the Garden of Eden—will provide the context for every person's life purpose. Every man and every woman will have a life purpose that fits within that charge.

Then notice what God did next:

> Now the Lord God had formed out of the ground all the wild animals and all the birds in the sky. He brought them to the man to see what he would name them; and whatever the man called each living creature, that was its name. (Gen. 2:19)

He gave Adam a specific task that fit within the general purpose. It is as if he said to Adam, "Adam, your life's purpose will be to care for and work my creation. That will keep you continually engaged forever, as there will be a never-ending set of tasks that will need to be done. So, let's begin. Your first job is to name the animals. I'll help. I'll bring them to you, and you name them."

The task of naming the animals resulted in Adam imposing his sense of organization on the creation and required a significant amount of creativity. Whereas before there was a certain amount of incoherence to creation—one could not even speak about the animals—now there was a higher level of organization.

Notice that...

1. Adam's life purpose was given to him by God, and it was to "work."
2. Adam's specific task—his immediate work—was given to him by God.
3. The job given to him required him to use his creativity and resulted in a more organized environment—man's unique imprint on creation.
4. God worked with Adam to complete the job.

We know that God made man in his own image. There are multiple ways that characteristics of humans mimic those of God. But the first way mentioned in the Bible has to do with work. One of the characteristics of God is that he is a worker. The Bible opens with the story of him working. We see him working at creating the universe and then resting from his work:

> By the seventh day God had finished the work he had
> been doing; so on the seventh day he rested from all
> his work. (Gen. 2: 2-3)

Since work is so important to God, when he made man, he made him to be a worker. Notice that before he created Eve, before there were spouses and families, before there was "church," before there were prophets or priests before there was Scripture, there was work. God gave Adam a job before he gave him a spouse.

And God chose to interact with man in the completion of the task that he gave to him. God worked with Adam to complete the task. His initial venue for relating to mankind was on the job!

> Since work is so important to God, when he
> made man, he made him to be a worker. Notice
> that before he created Eve, before there were
> spouses and families, before there was "church,"
> before there were prophets or priests, before
> there was Scripture, there was work.

It is as if God said to Adam, "Adam, if you want to talk to me and get to know me, the way to do that is to work with me. Lets work together.'

So, work becomes a foundational building block, not only of the rationale for man's existence but also as the venue in which God will relate to humanity. In these two passages, we see four fundamental precedents set:

Mankind's purpose—both lifetime as well as specific will be found within the context of work. God will give man—and, as we will see later, each person—a specific charge within the larger context of "working and caring for creation."

- Man's work will require him to use his gifts of creativity to create an ever-more-organized outcome.
- God will work with and interact with mankind within the context of his work.

> God did not create man only to worship him; he made man to work with him and thus relate to him!

The primary purpose of man's existence is to do work and to do it with God. At this point in the creation story, there are no businesses, as there are no other people. But as the Bible story unfolds and the world becomes populated, we see the emergence of businesses as one of the primary ways work is done.

These precedents set in the first moments of creation describe how God has worked with mankind throughout the ages. It doesn't matter if he is speaking to a people group (like Israel or the church) or if he is directing an individual (like Moses, Joshua, David, Paul, and Lydia). He gives man a charge: it always fits into the fundamental job of "keeping and working God's creation." Typically, it is a more specific task. Then he works with man in the completion of that task.

We see that same pattern—the pattern that he established in the very beginning—repeated over and over again in the pages of Scripture. Moses was given the charge to lead the people out of Egypt, and then God worked with him to do it. Joshua was given the charge to take the promised land from the inhabitants, and God worked with him to do it. David was given the charge to unite Israel into a unified kingdom, and God worked with him to do it. The list goes on and on with examples too numerous to include here.

Even in the New Testament, John was given the charge to prepare the way for Christ; Jesus himself was given the charge to usher in the Kingdom of God and was enabled to do so by the power of his Father. Paul was given the charge to take the Kingdom to the Gentiles and provided with the power of the Holy Spirit to do it.

The pattern is repeated so often that it is impossible to miss it. It is a fundamental way that God works with mankind. The apostle Paul makes it clear in his letter to the Ephesians:

> For we are God's handiwork, created in Christ Jesus to do good works, which God prepared in advance for us to do. (Eph. 2:10)

Work—and by extension, business—is so important to God that he has created "works" for each of us to do, and he prepared them way in advance of our being ready to do them. Just as he gave Adam the task of naming the animals and then worked with him on that task, so he gives each of us tasks to do and works with us to do them. It is how he designed his creation to operate.

While we are familiar with these grand movements of God and the great stories that describe them, we have missed one of the underlying truths: that the primary way God works with man is through our labor and the businesses that emerge from it. We have never seen that because we have never looked for it. The religious establishment, because it chooses to view business as a necessary evil, has had no reason to attempt to uncover the biblical view of business or the incredibly important role it plays in God's master plan.

If we can look at these Bible verses objectively, it is clear that God created man for work and, by extension, for business!

Thinking about this chapter...

1. What is the significance of the fact that God gave Adam work before he gave him a spouse and a family?

2. What are the implications of God relating to Adam in his work and working with him to accomplish the task Adam was given?

3. What Biblical examples can you find of the

precedent set in Genesis: God gives a person a task and then works with him to complete that task?

THREE

What Is a Biblical Business?

It does not take a lot of searching to notice the huge role that business and businesspeople play in the Bible story. Since work is the primary venue for God to interact with mankind, it only follows that business—the logical extension of work— is very important.

It is not so much that the Bible delivers commands to business people. There isn't a lot of "Thou shalt be honest in your business" kind of language, although there is some. Rather, the Bible portrays businesses as the cellular organizational unit for biblical economies and societies. We learn about biblical businesses more by seeing them in operation than by specific direction.

Most translations of the Bible use the term "household" to describe a business. Yet the religious establishment generally holds that "households" are another name for "family." While that fits our modern sensibilities, it is inaccurate. **It is a common mistake to think of a household as a family. The Bible actually says very little about families and family life. Ken Collins does a great job of articulating the issue:**

The Modern Nuclear Family

The concept of the nuclear family is about as old as the concept of the nuclear bomb. Even our most recent ancestors would find our definition of the word *family* very limiting, very odd, and perhaps even bizarre. Before World War II, a family included all living relatives, all ancestors, and even people who aren't legally related, such as brothers-in-law, sisters-in- law, third cousins, or even close friends. For instance, when my mother was growing up in the 1930s, she had an aunt who was really just a friend of the family by modern estimation.

Today, especially in politics, the real meaning of the word *family* is found more in whom it excludes rather than in whom it includes.

The word *family* appears increasingly in modern translations of the Bible, but neither biblical Greek nor biblical Hebrew possesses a word that means what we mean when we say, *family*! Where we speak of families, the Bible speaks of households. The translators put in the word *family*, not just to make their translation more accessible to us, but partly also to make our pocketbooks more accessible to them. There is a practical reason for this. In this day and age, the more a Bible translation appears to uphold family values, the more it will sell. What good is a Bible translation if no one reads it? And who will read it if no one buys it?

But we should also understand what the Bible means by *household*.

The Household of God

> So when we read in the Bible about households—or in more recent translations, about families—we must understand that twenty-first-century suburbia hadn't been invented yet. There were no household appliances, so there was a domestic staff. The household was both a family and a business; it included the family members, the upstairs maid, the gardener, the cook, the file clerk, the valet, the receptionist, the salesman, the stable hand, the swineherd, the housekeeper, the accountant, and the governess—and everyone lived together in one house. Well, that would have been a rather large household, but you get the idea. The members of the household were empowered to carry out the master's business. Imagine a farm in the American Midwest during the last century, such as Dorothy's home situation in the movie The Wizard of Oz, or the household in the British television series Upstairs Downstairs.[5]

Its my conviction that biblical households are really businesses. Here is why I have come to that conclusion:

1. They included employees.

Households were larger than families and included employees. For example, we know that Jacob was an employee of Laban and part of his household. Here is what he said to his father-in-law:

> It was like this for the twenty years I was in your *household.* I worked for you fourteen years for your two daughters and six years for your flocks, and you changed my wages ten times. (Gen. 31:41, italics added)

2. They included slaves.

Note what God said to the Israelites:

> For the generations to come every male among you who is eight days old must be circumcised, including those born in your *household* or bought with money from a foreigner—those who are not your offspring. (Gen. 17:12, italics added)

Those "bought with money" were, of course, slaves.

3. God provided households as a reward for obedience to Him.

> Because the midwives feared God, He established households for them. (Exod. 1:21, nasb)

4. Households could grow into very large entities.

Think about how large a household Abram must have had based on this verse:

> When Abram heard that his relative had been taken captive, he called out the 318 trained men born in his household and went in pursuit as far as Dan. (Gen. 14:14)

If there were 318 trained men who had been born in his household, how many additional untrained men would there have been? How many parents, older men, younger men, women, boys, and girls would there have been to have produced 318 trained men? It is not hard to envision a scenario that adds up to the thousands. While this is an example of a very large household, it follows that there were many of smaller size as well.

5. One could be a member of one household and also have his own.

Here is Jacob again speaking to Laban, his employer and father-in-law:

26

> The little you had before I came has increased
> greatly, and the Lord has blessed you wherever I
> have been. But now, when may I do something for
> my own *household*?" (Gen. 30:30, italics added)

Notice, too, that the Lord's blessing on the household
of Laban consisted of material wealth.

6. Households were, in part, about the acquisition and management of wealth.

Households had the survival of the family as their first
priority. However, as the household began to prosper,
they naturally began to spend time acquiring and
managing wealth. Note Genesis 30:30, the passage quoted
above, where the blessing on the household was an
increase in its wealth. Abraham's household extended to
the thousands—a dramatic concentration of wealth.

Like family businesses today, many grew beyond
survival and achieved success and prosperity. They
eventually evolved to focusing on expanding and
managing the wealth created by the household. God
chose to bless households, as he blessed Abraham and
Israel, by multiplying their wealth.

7. God blesses households by increasing their wealth.

Notice how the household of Potiphar was blessed
because of the presence of Joseph.

> From the time he put him in charge of his *household*
> and of all that he owned, the Lord blessed the
> *household* of the Egyptian because of Joseph. The
> blessing of the Lord was on everything Potiphar had,

both in the house and in the field. (Gen. 39:5, italics added)

8. They are often referred to as having people in them who were not part of the family.

Esau took his wives and sons and daughters and all the members of his *household*, as well as his livestock and all his other animals and all the goods he had acquired in Canaan, and moved to a land some distance from his brother Jacob. (Gen. 36:6, italics added)

9. One could have a household without having any family.

Review Genesis 14:14 above—the passage about Abraham and his 318 trained men. Abraham had a huge household and yet at that time had no family. While he was married to Sarah, he had no children at the time referred to in the story. It was not until he was an old man, with a household in the thousands, that he had children and began his family.

So, the biblical concept of household is larger and more expansive than that which is commonly understood as a family business today. A biblical business was organized around the work of the head of the household. While this "work" was often buying and selling or raising crops and livestock, it didn't always have a "business" application in the sense that we use the word today. This work could be raising sheep and cattle, like Abraham; working in stone and precious metals, like Bezalel; doing carpentry work, like Jesus;

making tents, like Paul; or managing the affairs of a political entity, like Herod and Pharaoh.

Some biblical businesses were not businesses by today's terms. We can think of the political rulers, for example, like Pharaoh, King David, and Herod, all having households in which the "business" was running the country or some part of it.

Let's create a definition. A biblical business is an organization of people often, but not always, centered around a set of people related by blood who work together to accomplish a specific God-given task within the greater purpose of applying creativity and organization to creation. A biblical business begins, from mankind's perspective, with the motivation for financial security and advantage.

> Definition: A biblical business is an organization of people often, but not always, centered around a set of people related by blood who work together to accomplish a specific God-given task within the greater purpose of applying creativity and organization to the creation. A biblical business begins, from mankind's perspective, with the motivation for financial security and advantage.

So, in today's terms, a biblical business could be for-profit or nonprofit; it could be a unit of government or an institution. These modern distinctions blur the issue by adding layers of distinction not known in biblical times. For our purposes, any of these entities can be termed a "biblical business." Were it not for the attraction of alliteration; I would use the term "financial enterprise" instead of biblical business. It's another way of thinking about the entity we are describing.

The business—or "household" in biblical terms—was the economic engine in the biblical narrative. The members of the household earned their living from the business of the household. Households—or biblical businesses—first provided a livelihood for their members. But they were so much more than that. Like every business, the household provided a place for people to relate to one another, to develop their individual potential, and to serve the larger community. Because work is so important to God, households are the cellular unit of God's organization of human society.

Jewish society was organized by God in this fashion: people groups—kingdoms—tribes—households.

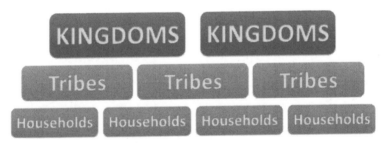

To learn what the good book has to teach us about business, we first must study biblical households.

Thinking about this chapter...

1. How often have you heard the biblical word "household" spoken of as if it meant "family?"

2. Review a couple of the verses that indicate that a household was not a family but rather a business.

3. Name some organizations of people that would fit the definition of a biblical business but that are not thought of as businesses today.

4. Since God created mankind for work and it is in work that he interacts with man, to what degree do you think biblical businesses are the cellular unit of Gods economy?

Biblical Business Profile: EC Group

Throughout this manuscript, you'll find real-life stories of businesses of various sizes and types that are striving to become Biblical businesses. These profiles provide a real- world application of the principles and concepts uncovered in the rest of the manuscript. Here is one such profile.

Tom Sudyk's story is a dramatic example of one of the manyways that God calls business people to the work he wants them to do.

EC group is composed of two business entities: an operation with about five employees in the US, and a wholly owned subsidary in India with approximately eighty employees. The company provides software developers in India who work directly for its US clients.

Following a number of years in law enforcement, Tom built and then sold a number of businesses, including a string of physical therapy clinics. In 1999, a couple of years after selling the business, he was searching for another business to start.

Looking back at this stage of his life, Tom reflects that he was a "cultural Christian." He went to church, taught Sunday school, and considered business to be one thing and church as something else. Money was the point at which the two intersected, and Tom, the businessperson, did his Christian duty by writing a check.

At this point, the Lord intervened in a dramatic way. Tom was sitting alone in his den when he heard an audible voice tell him "Go to India with Don." Don was Don Chapman, a director of Mission to India, a missionary organization. Don was an acquaintance; both men had kids on the same sports team.

One thing led to another, and Tom found himself in India, visiting five cities in ten days. Impressed with the reach of the mission organization and the tremendous opportunities in the developing nation, Tom decided to start a business in India. His motivation was twofold. He needed to have a business for personal and financial reasons, and he wanted to assist in the mission work. "It was easier to get money into the country through the business channel than by donations." He decided to "create an openly Christian company that blessed the people of India in culturally relevant ways."

A client who needed medical transcription services

appeared, as did a solid Christian woman who could run interference in India to create the business. Within ninety days, a business in India was created to do medical transcription for clients in the US.

At the time, the idea of an "openly Christian company that blessed the people" was a radical idea. Tom found himself as the spokesperson for a movement. He recognized that most of the people of his generation had the paradigm that the highest use of a business was to give money to Christian causes and that there was a divide between the sacred (church stuff) and secular (business). If the notion of a Kingdom business existed at all, it was defined as one in which the business was really a mask for the evangelical work that was its true purpose. The idea that a business could be openly Christian and profitable was not in the conversation.

He decided to invest in the younger generation and created internships in "business as mission" with a number of colleges. That led to an annual CEO conference, which he organized and presented for some years.

The business evolved. The medical transcription business was growing more complex, and the need for software developers emerged. Gradually, the company made the transition from one to the other and evolved a model whereby the Indian developers work directly for their stateside employers under the banner of EC Group.

The business has evolved into a family business in the mold of the biblical household. One of Tom's interns stuck with the company and spent ten years helping to develop the business and the concepts that empower it. He has moved on but still has influence on the company and is thought of as "almost an adopted son."

Tom's wife, Lynda, joined the company to oversee the bookkeeping. In addition, his son, Mike, is being groomed to take a senior role. All the Sudyk kids and spouses have been to India, and Tom recently arranged for Mike's wife to visit so that she would have a clear understanding of the family business.

At the same time, the Indian company continues to define what it means to be an "openly Christian company that blesses people."

"We want to treat everyone with compassion," Tom says. At the time of this interview, he has just received an e-mail notifying him of the death in an auto accident of the wife of one of his Indian employees. He had composed an e-mail to the employee, and both the COO and CFO of the Indian operation were planning to visit the family and spend time with them. Tom had already notified the client involved and allowed the grieving husband to take several weeks off to deal with the tragedy.

'It is times like these when your Christian witness becomes most valuable.'

The company has a ten-minute prayer time every day at 4:00 p.m. and a company-sponsored Bible study every two weeks—both of which are optional for the employees. It impacts the community with charitable events in which the employees engage.

For example, Little Hearts is an organization that serves the mentally and physically disabled. EC sends teams of people to spend time with the folks who are served by that organization. In addition, the company supports a school for slum children and actively looks for opportunities to spread their compassion and witness for Christ. You can view videos of this work at http://ecgroup-intl.com/about-us/ our-heartbeat/.

Looking ahead, Tom sees his role evolving to encompass focusing more on mentoring the next generation of leaders and inspiring others to embrace the vision.

FOUR

Abraham: A Biblical Business on Steroids

As the population increased, work necessarily morphed into a more sophisticated version, which today we call a "business." The Bible refers to these emerging organizations as "households." Households were formed as a result of individual families struggling for economic security. The head of the house found some work to do, and naturally, the whole family helped with that. As is the case today and ever since, some people were better at their business than others, and they inevitably attracted servants, slaves, and employees to expand the family business. Generally, these folks—the servants, slaves, and employees (the equivalent of today's employees)—lived in the same compound as the head of the household, and their families were considered to be part of the business as well.

One of the most successful of these early business people was Abraham, who, by no coincidence, was chosen by God to become the father of the special people group that he set aside to be dedicated to him—the Hebrews.

We get a glimpse of how large Abraham's business was in this passage, which describes a story in his life. Abraham was close to his nephew, Lot. Lot and his household had been captured by the enemy, and Abraham (then known as Abram) is going to go after them:

> When Abram heard that his relative had been taken captive, he called out the 318 trained men born in his *household* and went in pursuit as far as Dan. (Gen. 14:14, italics added)

Let's think about that. If there were 318 trained men who had been born in his household, how many untrained men must there have been in that household? How many boys who were too young, men who were too old, how many women and children? The size of Abraham's business would have incorporated thousands of people—a massive enterprise. Imagine the logistics involved in employing, organizing, and caring for thousands of people.

There would have been layers of management and specialization. Who selected and trained that fighting force of 318 men, for example? Someone probably was tasked with identifying the most likely candidates, acquiring the weapons, developing the training routines, and sharpening the skills of that group.

So, we get a glimpse of the first really big business in the Bible—Abraham's household.

> For those who hold that households are just another name for families, notice that Abraham had built a huge household and had no family beyond his wife, Sarah. He was, at this point in his life, childless.

The story of Abraham adds to our understanding of biblical businesses as we discover a powerful business principle. Let's call it "preparation for contingencies." How did those 318 trained men come into existence? Abraham must have identified the need for a fighting force to defend the business and its people in the event of an attack from outside. He was incredibly wealthy and ran a business with thousands of people who were dependent on the business for their livelihood. His holdings in crops, cattle, sheep, vineyards, etc. must have been extensive. As his business grew, so did the likelihood of a raid by an outside group, intent on taking some of what belonged to Abraham. Thinking ahead, Abraham would have decided to prepare for that eventuality and train and equip a fighting force to defend the business and its people.

This brings us to another biblical principle: specialization, which we see for the first time in

Abraham's business. Those 318 men were specialists in some aspect of the business—in this case, soldiering. Abraham, the first really big biblical businessperson, knew that some folks were better at some things than others and organized them to specialize in those things—a decidedly modern strategy.

Today we have lots of tools to help us assess a person's skills and aptitudes in order to put them in the right job. While Abraham did not have the sophisticated tools we employ today, he understood the principle and created this special force of 318 warriors.

In the bigger Bible story, God chose Abraham to be the father of his nation because of his great faith. The depth of that faith is revealed in one of the famous stories of the Bible. Here is the story:

Abraham and his wife, Sarah, were childless. Sarah grew beyond childbearing age and had given up on having children. But God, in fulfillment of his promise to make Abraham the father of a great nation, had miraculously intervened; and Sarah, in her old age, became pregnant with Isaac. The child was born and was destined to inherit both his father's business as well as the promise from God. As an only child of the couple, the bloodline would necessarily proceed through Isaac, and the promise that was made to his father was then extended to him.

In a test of Abraham's faith, God commands Abraham

to sacrifice Isaac, in the same way as he would sacrifice an animal. Abraham obeys. He leads Isaac off into the wilderness, builds an altar, places his only son on that altar, takes out his knife, and prepares to kill his son. God intervenes and stops Abraham, and Isaac lives and goes on to be another pivotal person in the Bible narrative. Abraham has passed the test and proven his faith and obedience.

The biggest lesson to add to our understanding of biblical business has to do with the intertwining of Abraham's business with the development of his faith. Clearly, he had an enormous depth of faith that expressed itself in his obedience to God's command to sacrifice Isaac. But how did he come to that level of faith?

Faith, in most people, grows over time. We generally begin our relationship with God with a small degree of faith (as large as a mustard seed) and over time add to our level of faith. It is interesting to note that God did not put Abraham to this incredibly difficult test of his faith until he was an elderly man and had developed a powerful faith.

How did Abraham, over the course of his life, develop such a legendary level of faith?

Often, people develop faith as they live through the successes and calamities of raising children. As a father, adoptive father, foster father, and grandfather, I can attest to that. But Abraham did not have children until his later years when his faith was well established.

Nor did he have access to any of the accouterments of modern-day religion, which we expect to be the mechanism to instill and develop faith: no churches, no Scripture, no pastors, and no church services. How, then, did he come to this legendary faith? Could it be that the venue in which he encountered God and grew to depend on and obey him was the same venue in which God showed himself to Adam? God set a precedent in the first few chapters of Genesis—it would be in work that God would interact with mankind. Understanding that, would it not be reasonable to expect that Abraham encountered God in the context of his business? Was it in Abraham's work, expressed in the more sophisticated version of is business, that Abraham encountered God, grew to know him, and came to a level of faith and obedience that is legendary?

> God set the precedent in the first few chapters of Genesis – it would be in work that God would interact with mankind. Understanding that, would it not be reasonable to expect that Abraham encountered God in the context of his business?

With no children in his family, running an enterprise of this size would have occupied the majority of Abraham's time. And it was there—in the relationships with his servants and slaves, in the countless thousands of conflicts he had to negotiate, in the myriad decisions he would have had to make, and in the thousands of conversations and interactions— that Abraham encountered God and developed his legendary faith. Abraham probably did what generations of Godly business people have done since -- and that they still do today -- when confronted with a problem, he would have gone to God for direction. It is not hard to imagine him in a scenario like this, praying to God: "God, the sheep in the north pasture are sickly. What should I do?" Or, "Lord, one of my shepherds has been lazy and not taking care of his sheep well. Should I fire him?" In the ebb and flow of problems and opportunities that define every business, Abraham went to God. And, in so doing, came to know God well and develop his historic faith. God showed up in Abrahams's business, just as he did with Adam.

Thinking about this chapter...

1. How big do you think Abraham's business must have been?

2. Since God set the precedent that he would give mankind tasks and then work with them to complete those tasks, is it reasonable to understand that God worked with Abraham to build the size of his business?

3. How did Abraham grow his faith? What was the venue for the testing and developing of faith?

4. What significance is there to the fact that Abraham grew a huge business and a legendary faith before he had a family?

FIVE

Rewards and Punishments

Following Abraham's life, the biblical narrative continues; and we follow the Hebrews, at this time defined by Jacob (Abraham's grandson) and his family, traveling to Egypt to survive a serious famine. The Hebrew tribe grew plentiful, and that began to worry Pharaoh, who didn't want them to become a threat to his rule. So, he calls two Hebrew midwives and tells them to kill all the male Hebrew babies.

> The king of Egypt said to the Hebrew midwives, whose names were Shiphrah and Puah, "When you are helping the Hebrew women during childbirth on the delivery stool, if you see that the baby is a boy, kill him; but if it is a girl, let her live." (Exod. 1:15–16)

The two midwives, however, decided not to comply. Pharaoh calls them on it, and they make up an excuse:

> The midwives, however, feared God and did not do what the king of Egypt had told them to do; they let the boys live. Then the king of Egypt summoned the midwives and asked them, "Why have you done this?

Why have you let the boys live?" The midwives answered Pharaoh, "Hebrew women are not like Egyptian women; they are vigorous and give birth before the midwives arrive." (Exod. 1:17–19)

God then rewards them for their obedience to him by growing their individual practices into businesses:

Because the midwives feared God, He established households for them. (Exod. 1:21, nasb)

It is not difficult to imagine the sequence of events. The two midwives were sole practitioners. However, God decided to bless them by turning their individual practices into larger businesses. In a practical sense, you can see them getting so busy that they had to employ others. As they did, their household (business) grew and prospered.

This story illustrates a fundamental principle of biblical businesses. When the head of the household is obedient and does good work, God often chooses to bless the household with both larger and more impactful work as well as an increase in worldly wealth

> When the head of the household is obedient and does good work, God often chooses to bless the household with both larger and more impactful work as well as an increase in worldly wealth.

We see it again in the story of Joseph. In the biblical narrative, God used Joseph to bring the Hebrews to Egypt to weather the famine. Joseph was sold as a slave by his brothers, who were jealous of him. He surfaces in

Potiphar's household. Potiphar was an important official in Pharaoh's government.

It is then that we see this principle again.

> From the time he put him in charge of his *household* and of all that he owned, the Lord blessed the *household* of the Egyptian because of Joseph. The blessing of the Lord was on everything Potiphar had, both in the house and in the field. (Gen. 39:5, italics added)

Recognizing Joseph's work ethic, integrity, and executive skill, he eventually put him in charge of everything. In today's language, he made him the CEO of his business. Note that the blessings came from God, on all the people and things that Potiphar owned, because of the presence and position of one of God's people: Joseph. Note also that Joseph was rewarded for his obedience to God with both an increase in his worldly wealth and a much larger and more substantial work.

This is a principle that God articulated very specifically:

> But remember the Lord your God, for it is he who gives you the ability to produce wealth, and so confirms his covenant, which he swore to your ancestors, as it is today. (Deut. 8:18)

Work, and by extension the organizations that do that work, is so important to God that He chose to bless the entire household of the ungodly Potiphar because of the actions of one of the household's members. If the basic function of a household is to do work and acquire wealth, then note once again that

God's blessing on the household consisted of increasing its worldly wealth.

This is probably nowhere more plainly taught than in the parable of the bags of gold (Matt. 10:14–30). We will discuss it in detail in a later chapter. For now, however, it is important to note that in the parable, the business owner went away and delegated a portion of his wealth to three employees. Those who increased his wealth were regarded with greater responsibilities and a closer relationship with the owner, while the one who did not increase the master's wealth was punished.

We see this principle repeated over and over in the Bible. Abraham was rewarded for his growing faith with an abundance of worldly wealth and a greater role in the kingdom. The two Hebrew midwives were rewarded for their obedience and good work with a larger business and more worldly wealth. Bezalel was rewarded for his good work with the responsibility to do even more important work—to decorate the temple. Joseph was rewarded for his obedience with a greater responsibility and worldly wealth, as he became the second most important person in Pharaoh's kingdom. In addition, the parable that Jesus taught on the bags of gold clearly teaches the same principle.

I could probably cite many other examples from the pages of the Bible, but I think we have discovered the principle. God is the same yesterday, today, and tomorrow. When we uncover a principle for how he deals with human beings, we can count on him continuing to evidence that principle in our dealing with him.

Consequences on the entire business

The story of Joseph and God's blessing on Potiphar's household signaled another characteristic of biblical businesses:

> God blesses or curses the entire household—all the family, slaves, servants, and employees— based on the actions of the head.

This is another central element of a biblical family business. Let us look at it more deeply.

Once again, Abraham gives us a model. His wanderings led him to Egypt, where he tried to protect himself by lying about Sarah, his wife. Sarah was very beautiful, and Abraham was afraid that someone would kill him to take Sarah as his or her own. So he told everyone that she was his sister.

> As he was about to enter Egypt, he said to his wife Sarai, "I know what a beautiful woman you are. When the Egyptians see you, they will say, 'This is his wife.' Then they will kill me but will let you live. Say you are my sister so that I will be treated well for your sake and my life will be spared because of you." When Abram came to Egypt, the Egyptians saw that Sarai was a very beautiful woman. And when Pharaoh's officials saw her, they praised her to Pharaoh, and she was taken into his palace. He treated Abram well for her sake, and Abram acquired sheep and cattle, male

and female donkeys, male and female servants, and camels. (Gen. 12:11–16)

While there is a lot to talk about in this passage, the one point I want to single out is contained in the next chapter:

> The Lord inflicted serious diseases on Pharaoh and his *household* because of Abram's wife Sarai. (Gen. 12:17, italics added)

So, here's the point: God punished Pharaoh's entire household—all the family, servants, slaves, and employees— because of Pharaoh's actions. Even if he was deceived and unknowingly took another man's wife as his, God would not let that go unpunished and chose to punish the entire household. One of the characteristics of the God of the Bible is this: He is consistent. If we can discover a pattern in how he interacts with mankind, we can expect that pattern to be repeated. And so it is with this issue of blessing or cursing the entire business for the actions of its head.

Since businesses are the places where God interacts with humanity, they are held to a higher standard.

> The ark of the Lord remained in the house of Obed- Edom the Gittite for three months, and the Lord blessed him and his entire *household.* (2 Sam. 6:11)

That higher standard works against them when one of their members sins, but it works for them when one of their members finds special favor in God's sight. It is not the family that is blessed; it is the entire household.

We can get a glimpse of this principle working today in many of our businesses. The actions of the CEO or owner will often have a positive or negative consequence on the entire company. If the owner makes good decisions and invests wisely, then the business and all the employees who gain their living from that business will prosper. On the other hand, the actions of the owner can be the reason for the demise of the business and the loss of employment for the employees.

It is easy for us to see the relationship between the business decisions of the owner and the implications on the employees. And there is some of that in the biblical narrative. For example, the household of the Pharaoh of Joseph's day was blessed because of the business decision of that Pharaoh to employ Joseph and to give him great responsibilities within his business.

The biblical story, however, also draws the cause-effect relationship from a moral and not a business perspective. For example, the household of the Pharaoh of Abraham's day was punished because of the moral actions on Pharaoh's part. There was nothing business-ish about the decision to take Sarah into his household.

We see God operating on this principle regarding other groups of people, over and above a business. For example, in the book of Joshua, we read the story of

Achan, a Hebrew who disobeyed God by taking some of the possessions of the people he defeated. His whole household was destroyed because of his sin.

> Then Joshua, together with all Israel, took Achan son of Zerah, the silver, the robe, the gold wedge, his sons and daughters, his cattle, donkeys and sheep, his tent and all that he had, to the Valley of Achor...Then all Israel stoned him and after they had stoned the rest, they burned them. (Josh. 7:24–26)

We see the principle in play with the various Hebrew kings. When the king was obedient to Jehovah, the people were blessed. And when the kings weren't, the people paid the price. Here is just one such incident:

> Go, tell Jeroboam that this is what the Lord, the God of Israel, says: I raised you up from among the people made you a leader over my people, Israel. I tore the kingdom away from the house of David and gave it to you but you have not been like my servant David, who kept my commands and followed me with all his heart, doing only what was right in my eyes. You have done more evil than all who lived before you. You have made for yourself other gods, idols made of metal; you have provoked me to anger and thrust me behind your back. Because of this, I am going to bring disaster on the house of Jeroboam. I will cut off from Jeroboam every last male in Israel—slave or free. I will burn up the house of Jeroboam as one burns dung, until it is all gone. Dogs will eat those belonging to Jeroboam who die in the city and the birds of the air will feed on those who die in the country. The Lord has spoken! (1 Kings 14:8–11)

If we were to extend this biblical principle to modern biblical businesses, we would clearly see a heavy responsibility on the owner and CEO to not only make wise business decisions but also to live a moral life. He

or she is held to a higher standard.

Thinking about this chapter...

1. What other biblical example can you name of God blessing or punishing the entire business as a result of the actions of the head?

2. What contemporary examples can you cite of the same principle?

3. To what degree are heads of organizations held to a higher standard today? Can you cite some examples?

Biblical Business Profile:
Howell Plumbing Supply

Duncan Stacey owns Howell Plumbing Supply, a Canadian company, and is committed to running it on a biblical basis. He came to this position in an uncommon way as a series of events unfolded in multiple areas of his life.

The company had its inception in the 1950s when it began by making enamel panels. That led to enameling sinks and bathtubs for the mobile home industry, which eventually led to selling toilets, sinks, bathtubs, and all the ancillary plumbing. And that led to a split-off company that eventually became Howell Plumbing Supply.

As an elementary school child, Duncan began babysitting for the owner's family. That led to part-time employment in the company, and that led to his first full-time job after graduating from high school. Through an unusual chain of events, at age twenty, Duncan became the owner of this small business. His new wife, Ann, quit her job as a nurse and came to work for the small business, which operated out of a large garage.

At first, the business grew, but it leveled off when Duncan had reached his capacity. Knowing he was at the limit of his time and resources, he decided he needed help to continue to grow the business. He brought in three equity partners, all of whom had worked in the business and helped nurture its growth. Three of the partners had worked together for over thirty-five years.

Early in this time, Duncan called himself a "nominal Christian." He thought of himself as a Christian, but he had no relationship with God and little knowledge of what being a Christian really meant. In another series of one thing leading to another, he and his wife engaged in a weekly Bible study for three years before coming to the point where he was ready to commit his life to Christ.

According to Duncan, "Life got better" following his conversion. He became a better father, treated his wife better, and became a better boss.

At one point in this process, Duncan and Ann decided to take a year off and search for God. They arranged for a year's sabbatical and took the kids off traveling the world for a year. He tells the story of how God spoke to him through his eight-year-old son. Sitting down to dinner in an RV outside of Paris, Jeff, his son, announced that they needed to pray for Tim, the adult son of a family friend. They did.

The next night, Jeff made the same request, and the family complied. A couple of months later, as they were checking in with their family back home on New Year's day, they learned that Tim had had a severe auto accident on the day that Jeff first asked them to pray for him. And the next day, Tim was facing the amputation of his foot; and Jeff, an eight-year-old child thousands of miles away, had asked the family to pray for him.

For years, Duncan thought the incident had to do with Jeff. Recently, he had one of those aha moments when he realized that it was God using Tim's misfortune and an eight-year-old child to communicate to Duncan that prayer counted and that God cared. That realization was huge in Duncan's life, and it caused a serious change in him.

Duncan returned to the business in 1988 as a totally com- mitted Christian. The business grew from under $100,000 to over $14 million in annual sales. Duncan's Christianity was a bit awkward for the other partners, but it never became a huge issue. However, in the last few years, the business stopped growing. In 2014, the partners evaluated their options and opted to sell out and retire.

At first, Duncan was ready to join them in selling the business and moving on. But a comment by a member of the Christian roundtable group of which

Duncan is a part challenged him to think about buying his partners out and turning the business into a biblically based business. Ann was initially opposed. However, after prayer and conversation, she came to the position where she wholeheartedly supported it. Recently, at age sixty-two, they mortgaged their home, borrowed money from the bank, and bought the partners out. After the deal was consummated, Duncan held a staff meeting and shared that he thought that it was what God wanted them to do. If he had not, there would have been many jobs lost. "Everybody knows that I am a Christian," Duncan says. 'And my employees are encouraged to hold me accountable to being a Christian.'

As Duncan works to instill biblical principles and practices in his business, he has developed a tentative personal mission statement: "to make the world and our lives better each day in spite of our faults and weaknesses." His values statement says the company labors: "to treat everyone in a Christ- like manner.'

Things are changing at Howell Pipe. In the last month, Duncan says he has had the opportunity to pray with four different employees—folks who were the same kind of nominal Christians that Duncan formerly considered himself to be.

On the prospect of going into debt at age sixty-two, Duncan says, "It is going to be a constant struggle. It is easy to say be bold when you are safe. If there is nothing to fear, there is no place for faith. It's a journey."

SIX

Relationships within Biblical Businesses

One of the most significant characteristics of biblical businesses is the nature of the relationship between the head of the business and the folks who work for him or her. There was an intense relationship between the head of the business and those in its employment beyond almost anything we see today.

In the last chapter, we saw that the entire business was blessed or punished based on the actions of its head. Likewise, the heads of the household had a responsibility for the folks in their employment that far exceeds anything we see around us today. Look at this verse, for example:

> A foreigner residing among you who wants to celebrate the Lord's Passover must have all the males in his *household* circumcised; then he may take part like one born in the land. No uncircumcised male may eat it. (Exod. 12:48, italics added)

I know; it sounds so strange. However, place it within the biblical narrative. The Hebrew people had been led out of Egypt, and God was shaping them to be his chosen people. No other people group in the world had the relationship with him that they had. No other people group had him leading them day and night. No other people group had the set of commandments and regulations, direct from God, that they had. God was separating them apart from all the other people in the world to be his chosen people—the people who would be a sign to everyone else of the existence of the living God and the people through whom the Messiah would come.

In addition, now he demands something from them—an act of obedience that sets them apart from the rest of the world; one that is personal, painful, and permanent; an act that requires faith and commitment on the part of the people. What was that act? Circumcision.

As he develops this command, he extends it to those non-Hebrews living among them. Note the role of the heads of households in it:

> A foreigner residing among you who wants to celebrate the Lord's Passover must have all the males in his *household* circumcised; then he may take part like one born in the land. No uncircumcised male may eat it. (Exodus 12:48 italics added)

It is hard to imagine a business owner today telling all his employees that they were going to be circumcised. That, of course, illustrates the depth of the relationship between the biblical heads of households and their employees.

With this much authority, it is only natural to expect that the heads of the business could speak for all the people involved with it. The following often-quoted passage from the Old Testament occurs after Moses has died and Joshua had led the Hebrews to the conquest of the promised land. The people who had inhabited the land before them have been pretty much driven out and defeated, and the land had been divided up among the twelve tribes. Joshua grows old and assembles the leaders of the tribes to a last conference. In it, he reflects on how God had led them to the point where they are now. He issues his final challenge to the people:

> But if serving the Lord seems undesirable to you, then choose for yourselves this day whom you will serve, whether the gods your ancestors served beyond the Euphrates or the gods of the Amorites, in whose land you are living. But as for me and my *household*, we will serve the Lord. (Josh. 24:15, italics added)

There is the head of the household speaking for all his family, slaves, and employees.

To illustrate the degree to which the heads of biblical family businesses had influence over the members of the household, we need to visit some passages from the New Testament— the story of Jesus and the expansion of Christianity. Here is the story.

Christ has lived, died, been resurrected, and has ascended into heaven. The apostles are now left with the charge to "go into all the world, making disciples..." (Matt. 28:19).

Paul and Luke have traveled to Philippi and have sat down to speak with a group of women, one of whom was a prosperous businessperson named Lydia. Lydia responded to Paul's message. See what happens next:

> When she and the members of her *household* were baptized, she invited us to her home. "If you consider me a believer in the Lord," she said, "come and stay at my house." And she persuaded us. (Acts 16:15, italics added)

Lydia, the owner and proprietor of a business selling purple cloth, believes and converts to Christianity, and her whole household follows her. Once again, we see this phenomenon— the entire group of family, servants, slaves, and employees followed the actions of the head. If God holds businesses as the primary place for people to interact with him, it comes as no surprise that the entire enterprise encountered Him and believed together. This phenomenon occurs so often that it almost becomes standard operating procedure.

Here is another occurrence. Paul and Silas are accused of advocating unlawful customs and are beaten and thrown in prison. In the middle of the night, there was a miraculous earthquake, which threw the doors of the prison open and unshackled the prisoners. The jailer, who had been sleeping, woke up and saw the doors of the prison open. He panicked and prepared to kill himself, knowing his superiors would hold him accountable for the prisoners.

Paul intervened. The jailer immediately believed. Read what happens next:

> At that hour of the night the jailer took them and washed their wounds; then immediately he and all his *household* were baptized. The jailer brought them into his house and set a meal before them; he was filled with joy because he had come to believe in God—he and his whole *household*. (Acts 16:33–34, italics added)

This describes the conversion of the jailer who witnessed Paul's miraculous release from prison. The whole household— family, slaves, servants, and employees—chose to believe with him at the same time.

There are many things to talk about in this passage, but the one thing I want to emphasize is the degree to which the opinions and actions of the head of the household—the jailer—had on the members of his household.

Here is yet one more example. This time, we find Paul in Corinth, and he approaches the synagogue leader with the gospel. Here is what happens next:

> Crispus, the synagogue leader, and his entire *household* believed in the Lord; and many of the Corinthians who heard Paul believed and were baptized. (Acts 18:8, italics added)

This is yet another in the string of examples of the head of the household leading the way in believing in

Christ and the entire household following his example.

The biblical narrative contains stories like these in which the head of the household, the equivalent of today's business owner, makes some decision and the entire household—all the family, slaves, servants, employees—follow him or her in that decision. Whether it is to be circumcised, follow Jehovah, or commit to Christ, the entire business follows the lead of the owner.

That speaks to the depth of the relationship between the owner and those in his employ as well as the culture that existed in these businesses. While some of this can be accounted for by the larger cultural mores of the society— that's what every household employee was expected to do— still, it reveals a unique characteristic for the businesses of the time.

It is hard to see that relationship without wondering about how the owners managed to develop that kind of following. What did they do to create the kind of allegiance and respect that we see demonstrated in the passages noted above? How were they able to develop a culture within the business that would prompt the employees to follow the decisions of the owner to such a degree that they would be circumcised or follow Christ? More importantly, if we decide to model some of our business practices after the biblical model, then how would we create a culture within our businesses that would engender a level of respect and commitment that would begin to approach the biblical example?

It is not hard to imagine a business owner being intimately connected with the lives of his/her employees. Attending graduations, weddings, and funerals would be part of the routine. Lunches and dinners together, business picnics, and family outings would also be on the agenda. But probably most importantly, the owner would take the time to get to know each employee deeply, understand their aspirations and problems, and be aware of their ups and their downs.

The role of family in the business

Not all biblical businesses employed the family's children. For example, Abraham built a huge business before he had children. Moses, in the middle third of his life, spent forty years in a sheep-raising business and only had one child, who is barely mentioned in Scripture. There is no mention of any children or family in the story of the two Hebrew midwives who were given businesses. Jacob worked in Laban's business as an employee. His children were not a part of that business. These were probably the exceptions, however, not the rule.

As you might expect, there are some passages that mention teenagers working in the family business. The young man who later was to become King David is first pictured in the fields caring for the inventory in his father's sheep- raising business. (1 Sam. 16:8–13). When Joseph was sold to the slave traders who took him to Egypt, he and his brothers were doing the same thing.

Beyond that, one has a sense that there is a different attitude toward children in the Bible. Children were seen as having a responsibility toward a larger purpose—the prosperity of the entire household. In other words, they were expected to contribute at a very young age to the well-being of the household.

> Life was more about the business than it was about the children's individual aspirations and gratifications.

Spouses, at least in some cases, were a part of the business as well. Notice that in this famous Proverb, the wife is being praised, at least in part, for her actions on behalf of the business. I have included some of the pertinent parts of this passage below:

> A wife of noble character who can find? She is worth far more than rubies. She considers a field and buys it; out of her earnings she plants a vineyard. She sees that her trading is profitable, and her lamp does not go out at night.
>
> In her hand she holds the distaff and grasps the spindle with her fingers.
>
> She opens her arms to the poor and extends her hands to the needy.
>
> She makes linen garments and sells them, and supplies the merchants with sashes.

She watches over the affairs of her household and does not eat the bread of idleness. (Prov. 31:10, 16, 18–20, 24, 27)

Thinking about this chapter...

1. If we decide to model some of our business practices after the biblical model, then how would we create a culture within our businesses that would engender a level of respect and commitment that would begin to approach the biblical example?

2. Clearly, the Bible narrative indicates a very strong relationship between the business's employees and the head of the business. What would be some modern- day examples of that same principle applied?

3. How does the Bible treat children and businesses?

4. What do you make of the fact that several businesses in the New Testament were converted all at one time?

SEVEN

Biblical Businesses Have Spiritual Significance

Not only are family businesses the cellular unit of the economy and society in the Bible but they are also so important to the God of the Bible that they take on spiritual significance.

First, lets explore the concept of spiritual significance.

Millions of people feel an emptiness and recognize it as a lack of spiritual growth on their part. So, they search for something spiritual to fill that void. Unfortunately, many are searching in the wrong place, their energies being diffused by an errant understanding of spirituality.

I was recently contacted by the publishers of a Web site devoted to exploring spiritual issues for businesspeople.

"Would I like to contribute some content?" they wanted

to know. Before I answered, I viewed the site. The first article discussed the spiritual feelings the author experienced during a walk in the forest. Another discussed the spiritual connection he felt with other humans as a result of an exercise in a seminar. All the other articles repeated the same themes. Spirituality, according to these writers, was an experience of solitude, emotion, or a sense of one's similarity to other human beings, or even a sense of being part of nature.

I declined the invitation. I am not quite sure what the site was about, but I know it wasn't spirituality.

The site was another example of the trend to dumb down spirituality. Sort of like the political correctness trend. The more general and vague a concept is, the more people you can include in it and the less meaning and power it has. Everyone subscribes to the concept of freedom, for example. But you see a considerable drop-off when you link it to personal responsibility.

Spirituality in these times has come to mean, in the common usage, almost anything the speaker wants it to mean. Do you have a warm feeling as the result of a laugh you shared with someone? Must be spiritual. Do you feel a little introspective while out on a sailboat? Must be a spiritual experience. Sense a bit of a connection with another human being? You must truly be spiritual soul mates.

These are all valid and valuable moments. However,

while all these experiences and others of similar nature may be warm, pleasant, and even intuitive, they aren't spiritual. To call them spiritual is to detract from that which really is spiritual and to distract people from the search for the genuine article. Provide people with a cheap substitute, and you often knock them off the quest for the better original. The ice cream store won't sell very much Häagen-Dazs, for example, if they give away Dairy Queen.

So, if these kinds of experiences aren't spiritual, what is? Let's start at the source. There is a body of knowledge concerning things spiritual available to us. It's contained in the Bible. The information concerning things spiritual in the Bible is quite clear, consistent, and pretty simple. God is spirit. Anything having to do with God is spiritual.

God has, for his own reasons, lopped off and spread around parts of the spirituality that originated with him. There are, for example, totally spiritual beings. The Bible refers to them as angels and demons. Also, God has imbued part of his spirituality into human beings. There is a spiritual part of every human being. It is that part of us that lives on after our physical body dies. It is partially characterized by its hunger for communication with its Creator.

We can all relate to that. There are probably few human beings who haven't had, in moments of solitude and reflection, a sense of the infinite, a hunger to contact God. That is our spirit hungering for communication with its maker. It is a predictable, naturally occurring event. We are all some part spiritual. That part longs for completion by communion with its maker, in the same way that a male instinctively searches for a female that will complement and complete him and vice versa. One of the most natural things in the world is to search for God. That is spiritual.

So, spiritual has to do with our search for communion with God. We grow spiritually when we move toward that relationship with our maker or become more intimate with him. Anything else, all the other prescriptions for spiritual growth, miss the mark and detract our spirits from their instinctive destination.

Let us use this understanding and apply it to some commonly considered "spiritual" moments. For example, when we experience a feeling of connectedness to other human beings, that is not spiritual. Dogs, chimpanzees, and porpoises recognize a similarity to others of their species as well. That's just one member of a species recognizing another. However, when we experience a hunger for or communication with God, that is spiritual.

You feel a bond with another person; you are somehow mystically drawn to that person. Is that spiritual? No. In a world with billions of people, it's only natural that some are going to rub you the wrong way and that with some you are going to feel an affinity. That's just natural. It's not spiritual.

On a solitary hike into the mountains, you stop for a rest at a scenic place and are awed by the grandeur of what you see. Is that spiritual? Could be. The physical beauty and the feeling it inspires are natural, not spiritual. But if that beauty and those emotions cause you to reflect on the nature of God and your place in His scheme or perhaps to offer a short prayer, then that part of the experience is spiritual.

Having established what "spiritual" means, the question now is in what ways do biblical family businesses have spiritual significance?

In the beginning

Remember, in the very beginning; God created work as the place in which he would interact with mankind. That is not to say that an individual cannot find God in any of a limitless number of places and situations. However, there is something special about work and business in God's eyes.

If being spiritual is about finding God and interacting with him, then the workplace in general, and businesses, in particular, have spiritual significance because it is there where he consistently interacts with humankind.

> Businesses have spiritual significance, because it is in them where God interacts with mankind.

A conduit for biblical commands

The command in the Old Testament times to be circumcised and to cause others to be circumcised was given, in part, to the households—the biblical businesses.

> Because God ordained work—and by extension, business—as the place where he would interact with mankind, it is very consistent to see him using this entity—the biblical business—as the conduit for his commands.

Truly, the biblical business has a role in God's eyes far bigger and deeper than just providing an income to its stakeholders.

En masse

In the New Testament, biblical businesses became Christians en masse, indicating the potential for spiritual impact in the business. In chapter 9, we'll examine this issue in detail. For now, just note that there are multiple examples of whole households—the entire business—being converted to Christ at one time.

When it came time for Jehovah to send his Messiah and begin to draw people to him, he chose, at least in part, to use the business as the venue in which to do so. The most common meeting places for the early

Christians were the homes of business people. God very often converted the entire business at one time, and then that group of people began to function not only as a business but additionally as a church. That is spiritual significance.

Spiritual gifts

There is a concept taught in the Scriptures that we need to explore to understand this point. "Spiritual gifts" are special abilities distributed by God among his people that are a little bit of God in us. This concept is illustrated in the Old Testament and plainly taught in the New. For example, here is a passage from the book of First Corinthians. This is a letter that the apostle Paul sent to the Christians living in the city of Corinth. In it, he deals with a variety of practical and theological issues, one of which is the concept of spiritual gifts. Here is what he said:

> Now about the gifts of the Spirit, brothers and sisters, I do not want you to be uninformed. You know that when you were pagans, somehow or other you were influenced and led astray to mute idols. Therefore, I want you to know that no one who is speaking by the Spirit of God says, "Jesus be cursed," and no one can say, "Jesus is Lord," except by the Holy Spirit. There are different kinds of gifts, but the same Spirit distributes them. There are different kinds of service, but the same Lord. There are different kinds of working, but in all of them and in everyone it is the same God at work. Now to each one the manifestation of the Spirit is given for the common good. To one there is given through the Spirit a message of wisdom, to another a message of knowledge by means of the same Spirit,

> to another faith by the same Spirit, to another gifts
> of healing by that one Spirit, to another miraculous
> powers, to another prophecy, to another distinguishing
> between spirits, to another speaking in different kinds
> of tongues, and to still another the interpretation of
> tongues. All these are the work of one and the same
> Spirit, and he distributes them to each one, just as he
> determines. (1 Cor. 12:1–11)

So here is the idea. God distributes these special attributes among his people to accomplish some of the things that he wants to be accomplished—work that he has created for mankind to do.

So, what is the venue in which humanity exercises his spiritual gifts? You guessed it—business. While not the only place for the use of spiritual gifts, it is the first place. The first two recorded instances of spiritual gifts both take place in the context of biblical businesses!

Here is the first. Joseph (yes, the Joseph of the coat of many colors), Abraham's great-grandson, is sold by his older brothers into slavery. His slave masters take him to Egypt, where he finds himself working in Potiphar's household. He is unjustly accused of making a pass at Potiphar's wife and is thrown into jail. There he encounters a couple of other prisoners who both had disturbing dreams. Joseph claims that he can interpret the dreams and attributes his ability to interpret the dream as belonging to God, thus attributing that ability to what we later would see is a spiritual gift. Here is the passage:

> Then Joseph said to them, 'Do not interpretations belong to God? Tell me your dreams.' (Gen. 40:8)

Alas, Joseph remains in prison until Pharaoh has a dream, and the prisoner for whom Joseph interpreted the dream remembers him and recommends him to Pharaoh. In front of Pharaoh, Joseph again attributes his ability to interpret dreams to God:

> Pharaoh said to Joseph, "I had a dream, and no one can interpret it. But I have heard it said of you that when you hear a dream you can interpret it." "I cannot do it," Joseph replied to Pharaoh, "but God will give Pharaoh the answer he desires." (Gen. 41:15–16)

Joseph then correctly interprets Pharaoh's dream and is put in charge of the project of preparing the country for seven years of famine, a very business-ish task. So, in this first recorded instance of spiritual gifts, the application is a very business-ish task, and Joseph becomes the CEO of Pharaoh's business.

The next instance of spiritual gifts is also a businessperson: Bezalel. Here is the story. The Hebrews have left Egypt, being led into the wilderness by Moses. They have camped at the base of Mt. Sinai, and Moses has received the Ten Commandments from God. But God's directions to the Hebrews are far more detailed and exhaustive than just the Ten Commandments. Pages and pages of the Bible are devoted to rendering the specific rules that God delivers to the Hebrews. The whole of this is later referred to as the "Law of Moses," or shorthand, just "the Law."

As part of this, God describes in intricate detail the tent that is to be the place where Moses and Aaron and the new priests will offer sacrifices on behalf of the people. It will contain the Ark of the Covenant. Here is a passage to give you an idea of the level of detail in God's commandments. In this passage, God is describing how he wants the lampstands made:

> Make a lampstand of pure gold. Hammer out its base and shaft, and make its flowerlike cups, buds and blossoms of one piece with them. Six branches are to extend from the sides of the lampstand—three on one side and three on the other. Three cups shaped like almond flowers with buds and blossoms are to be on one branch, three on the next branch, and the same for all six branches extending from the lampstand. And on the lampstand there are to be four cups shaped like almond flowers with buds and blossoms. One bud shall be under the first pair of branches extending from the lampstand, a second bud under the second pair, and a third bud under the third pair— six branches in all. The buds and branches shall all be of one piece with the lampstand, hammered out of pure gold. (Exod. 25:31–36)

This kind of detailed description of how to make everything in the tabernacle goes on for pages. Clearly, Moses and the Hebrews have a huge challenge in front of them: how to put all of this together, exactly as God said he wanted it.

There is a pattern here. From where did the work give to Adam come? God created it and gave it to him. And from where did the work given to Moses come? God created it and gave it to him. In the Garden, the work was to name the animals. Now it is to construct the tabernacle and all the furnishings exactly as he wanted.

This task would seem insurmountable. But in the pattern that began in the Garden of Eden and continues throughout the Bible, God provides a way to get this done. In the creation story, he brought the animals to Adam. In the story of Bezalel, he works with his people once again:

> Then the Lord said to Moses, "See, I have chosen Bezalel, son of Uri, the son of Hur, of the tribe of Judah, and I have filled him with the Spirit of God, with skill, ability and knowledge in all kinds of crafts— to make artistic designs for work in gold, silver and bronze, to cut and set stones, to work in wood, and to engage in all kinds of craftsmanship." (Exod. 31:1–6)

How was Moses to accomplish this huge task? Delegate it to a businessperson, one whom God had selected and filled with the necessary skills, ability, and knowledge to do it. Notice that the gifts poured into Bezalel were primarily exhibited in the marketplace.

While this particular application had spiritual implications, the craftsmanship that Bezalel brought to the task was developed in doing work for others in the marketplace of the time. It is not hard to imagine Bezalel being commissioned by the folks around him to create pieces of jewelry and household items. He may even have had a shop and offered his work for sale. He was probably an independent businessperson.

He was not a prophet, a teacher, or a priest. God chose an artisan, a worker with gold, silver, and bronze, to do this monumental task. God equipped this businessperson with a supernatural power to "engage in all kinds of craftsmanship."

Moses himself said that Bezalel had a spiritual gift and that it was for use in the marketplace. Look:

> Then Moses said to the Israelites, "See, the Lord has chosen Bezalel son of Uri, the son of Hur, of the tribe of Judah, and he has filled him with the Spirit of God, with wisdom, with understanding, with knowledge and with all kinds of skills—to make artistic designs for work in gold, silver and bronze, to cut and set stones, to work in wood and to engage in all kinds of artistic crafts. And he has given both him and Oholiab son of Ahisamak, of the tribe of Dan, the ability to teach others. He has filled them with skill to do all kinds of works engravers, designers, embroiderers in blue, purple and scarlet yarn and fine linen, and weavers—all of them skilled workers and designers. (Exod. 35:30–35)

Notice that in both of these first two examples of spiritual gifts, the gift has tentacles that reach into the world of work and businesses specifically. Joseph's gift of interpreting dreams lands him the position of CEO of Pharaoh's household, and Bezalel's gift of craftsmanship was honed in his business.

A little bit of thoughtfulness will bring us to a similar conclusion when we consider the New Testament passage on spiritual gifts quoted above. Note that the gifts are given for the common good.

> This spiritual significance underscores the special place that businesses have in the Bible. They are not just entities that provide a living for their stakeholders. They are ascribed special spiritual significance in the eyes of the God.

He blesses and curses them, he interacts with humanity through them, he distributes his gifts to be used in them, and he delivers the gospel to them.

He blesses and curses them, he interacts with mankind through them, he distributes his gifts to be used in them, and he delivers the Gospel to them.

And the pattern repeats: God creates the work and then uses that task to interact with humanity in accomplishing it. Work—and by extension, business— is so important to God that he chose a businessperson to lead every major movement in the Bible.

While the full story for many of these examples is beyond the scope of this book, here is a small sampling of the business people who were chosen to lead major movements in the Bible:

Abraham

One of the most successful of all biblical business people, he headed an enterprise of thousands and was chosen to be the father of the special people group later known as the Israelites.

Jacob
A third-generation business owner, he fathered what was to become the twelve tribes of Israel.

Moses
In the business of raising sheep and was chosen to lead the Hebrews out of Egypt and into the promised land.

Saul
The first king of the Hebrews, was working for his father in his business when his life was interrupted, and he was called to be king.

David
Employed by his father in a family business, he was chosen to be the second king of Israel; he consolidated the kingdom and wrote most of the Psalms.

Jesus
A small businessperson, he was a carpenter for the majority of his adult life.

Peter
A small businessperson, he had a fishing business when he was called by Christ to become an apostle, and he became one of the highly visible leaders of the early church.

Paul
Was a tentmaker, a sole proprietor, who led the advance of Christianity into most of the known world following the death and resurrection of Jesus.

Let's consolidate what we have learned. Biblical businesses are so important to God that he ascribes special spiritual significance to them.

They are, in part, how he chooses to deliver the command to be circumcised. They are the primary venue for the expression of spiritual gifts. God blesses or curses the entire business for the moral lapses or virtues of the business leaders. When it came time to expand the church, he chose to convert whole businesses at one time. He chose business as the venue to build and develop great leaders in the Bible.

Thinking about this chapter...

1. Respond and react to this statement: If being spiritual is about finding God and interacting with him, then the workplace in general and businesses, in particular, have spiritual significance because it is there where he consistently interacts with humankind.

2. To what degree were you aware that the first two incidences of the use of spiritual gifts were both business applications?

3. Respond and react to this statement: This spiritual significance underscores the special place that businesses have in the Bible. They are not just entities that provide a living for their

stakeholders. They are ascribed special spiritual significance. God blesses and curses them, he interacts with mankind through them, he distributes his gifts to be used in them, and he delivers the gospel to them.

4. What are implications of the fact that God used a businessperson to lead almost every major movement in the Bible?

Biblical Business Profile: VFP

Daron has a business which creates automated sales systems for the health and fitness industry. His seventeen-person business is completely virtual— everyone works out of his or her home. He and Mario, his partner, got their first customer in 2002 and today serve 1,600 locations in fifteen countries.

It was not easy. Mario was running the physical therapy for a hospital health care system, and Daron was running the health and fitness centers for that same system. They were both entrepreneurial types and decided to go into business together.

Even though neither were technology people, the two decided to build what

is essentially a technology business. They both wanted to create a business that reflected their faith and decided the company would tithe from the company's revenues. They sold stock to their family and friends and launched. They acquired their first customer in 2002, a few more in 2003, and achieved their first big break in 2004.

One of their unique advantages is a patented 3-D avatar that visually shows someone their body's potential for change. Based on an exercise and nutrition regime, the technology also predicts what those changes will be and personally predicts the likelihood of getting diabetes, heart disease, stroke, and cancer as well as the specific reduction of those risks based on lifestyle changes.

Daron was raised in a Christian home and felt strongly that he wanted to honor God with his life. The business was a natural extension of that motivation. Daron reflects, "In business, if you are just doing it for the sake of profit, there is no self-satisfaction, no higher purpose. It's just another month to hit budget and hit goal. What is the meaning in all ofthat?"

Daron attributes his Truth@Work Christian Executive Roundtable Group for giving him insights into how to mold his operation into a God-honoring business.

"The group has given me more concrete ways to implement core values. It has given me a framework and a focus for reflectingmyvalues."

One example has to do with his attitude toward his employees: "I want every single employee to be better off for having been a part of my organization and knowing me, regardless of how long they are here. I want every employee to be able to say that this organization has positively impacted their life.'

Here is an example. He had a difficult employee

whose behavior was detrimental to the company. "I'm sure anyone else would have terminated him," Daron says. But because he saw the organization as a means of impacting people for eternity, he prayed about it, talked it over with his roundtable group, and concluded that the employee had been emotionally wounded somewhere in his life. Instead of firing him, Daron drove the three and a half hours to his home and spent several hours with him. He first shared with the employee that he cared for him, shared his biblical worldview with him, and then addressed the specific work issues that were problematic.

The outcome? The employee has made a dramatic improvement in all the problem areas and has become a much more effective employee. Daron continues to pray for him.

Daron attributes his largest contract specifically to God's doing. Here is the story. He had been working on a large potential customer on and off for ten years and had gotten nowhere. Last year, he was attending a trade show in Chicago and received an e-mail from one of his customers, setting up a meeting with him and a representative of the potential customer. Four days later, Daron was in San Francisco, presenting to the company's board. Within two weeks, he had a verbal commitment from the company to use his system. A few months later, he was in over four hundred different locations for that company.

"They are a billion-dollar company," Daron says. "For them to move that quickly and completely with my little company is miraculous.'

Looking ahead, Daron is most excited about the potential to provide an opportunity to more people to work from home. "I'd love to have a thousand moms and dads working for me who can invest in their family's lives and not have to commute to work."

EIGHT

What Jesus Said about Biblical Businesses

Jesus **rarely taught** specifically about households but instead used them as the backdrop or the venue for some of his parables and teachings. We learn about his views on households by inference. Let us look at some passages that quote things that he said.

> It is enough for students to be like their teachers, and servants like their masters. If the head of the house has been called Beelzebub, how much more the members of his *household!* (Matt. 10:25, italics added)

In this passage, Jesus is commenting on the impact of the head of the household on the members of that household. If the head of the household is evil (Beelzebub is another name for Satan), so will be the members of that household. Note that he talked about households, not families. Households (businesses), not families, were his frame of reference.

> Jesus knew their thoughts and said to them, "Every kingdom divided against itself will be ruined, and every city or *household* divided against itself will not stand." (Matt. 12:25, italics added)

Notice the progression in his thinking: kingdoms, cities, and households. Notice that he did not say "kingdoms, cities, households, and families." In Jesus's view, households were seen as the smallest, most fundamental organizational unit of society. They were the cellular unit.

> Who then is the faithful and wise servant, whom the master has put in charge of the servants in his *household* to give them their food at the proper time? (Matt. 24:45, italics added)

Once again, notice that Jesus uses the household as the context from which to deliver a teaching about servants. There is the understanding that the household is the primary organizational unit in society. It is the cellular unit. His teachings about service and stewardship are set in the context of a household. Note that the household in this passage is large enough to have multiple servants and levels of management. The faithful and wise servant would be called a manager in todays world.

Note also that Jesus introduced himself to three of his disciples by first blessing their business.

> One day as Jesus was standing by the Lake of Gennesaret, the people were crowding around him and listening to the word of God. He saw at the water's

edge two boats, left there by the fishermen, who were washing their nets. He got into one of the boats, the one belonging to Simon, and asked him to put out a little from shore. Then he sat down and taught the people from the boat. When he had finished speaking, he said to Simon, "Put out into deep water, and let down the nets for a catch." Simon answered, "Master, we've worked hard all night and haven't caught anything. But because you say so, I will let down the nets." When they had done so, they caught such a large number of fish that their nets began to break. So they signaled their partners in the other boat to come and help them, and they came and filled both boats so full that they began to sink. When Simon Peter saw this, he fell at Jesus' knees and said, "Go away from me, Lord; I am a sinful man!" For he and all his companions were astonished at the catch of fish they had taken, and so were James and John, the sons of Zebedee, Simon's partners. (Luke 5:1–10)

Jesus often taught by using parables. A parable is a story that is constructed to engage the audience and get them thinking about a lesson that applies to their situation. Think of them like the biblical version of a case study. One of the most well-known of these parables is known as the parable of the talents. The translation of the story has traditionally been a bit unfortunate. The word that is translated as "talent" refers to a bag of money—a substantial amount, equivalent to about twenty years of a day laborer's wages. Therefore, the parable is about money. However, many people focus on the word "talent" and think the story is about one's abilities. While the principles being taught can certainly be applied in that way, the heart of the story is about a

business owner delegating authority for portions of his wealth to senior members in his business.

Lets read the story. Here is the story in Jesus's own words:

Again, it will be like a man going on a journey, who called his servants and entrusted his wealth to them. To one he gave five bags of gold, to another two bags, and to another one bag, each according to his ability. Then he went on his journey. The man who had received five bags of gold went at once and put his money to work and gained five bags more. So also, the one with two bags of gold gained two more. But the man who had received one bag went off, dug a hole in the ground and hid his master's money. After a long time the master of those servants returned and settled accounts with them. The man who had received five bags of gold brought the other five. "Master," he said, "you entrusted me with five bags of gold. See, I have gained five more." His master replied, "Well done, good and faithful servant! You have been faithful with a few things; I will put you in charge of many things. Come and share your master's happiness!" The man with two bags of gold also came. "Master," he said, "you entrusted me with two bags of gold; see, I have gained two more." His master replied, "Well done, good and faithful servant! You have been faithful with a few things; I will put you in charge of many things. Come and share your master's happiness!" Then the man who had received one bag of gold came. "Master," he said, "I knew that you are a hard man, harvesting where you have not sown and gathering where you have not scattered seed. So I was afraid and went out and hid your gold in the ground. See, here is what belongs to you." His master replied, "You wicked, lazy servant! So you knew that I harvest where I have not sown and gather where I have not scattered seed? Well then, you should have put my money on deposit with the bankers, so that when I returned I would have received it back with interest. So take the bag of gold from him and give it to the one who has ten bags. For

whoever has will be given more, and they will have an
abundance. Whoever does not have, even what they
have will be taken from them. And throw that
worthless servant outside, into the darkness, where
there will be weeping and gnashing of teeth." (Matt.
10:14–30)

The story is clearly about a head of a household
delegating authority for his money to his servants and
then holding them responsible for their stewardship of
that money. It is about money and the household
servants' responsibility to invest that wisely.

What can we learn about biblical businesses from it?

Let's begin with the realization that the parable exists
at all. Jesus, it turns out, is concerned about business,
about money, about the appropriate investment of it,
and about individuals' accountability to make good
decisions about it. The story is about bags of gold!
Business, in the sense of the acquisition of worldly
wealth, is important in the Bible. We saw it in the Old
Testament from the moment of creation and
throughout the biblical narrative, and now we see it in
the teachings of Jesus.

The parable underscores the notion that households
were, in large part, about the acquisition and
management of wealth. They exist in the worldly realm
to expand their affluence and influence. And God is
interested in the mechanics of how that is done.

The three "managers" were each entrusted with a

portion of their boss's wealth and expected to invest that wisely. The managers were authorized to do whatever they wanted with that portion of their boss's wealth. From the perspective of the managers, they were expected to be good stewards of their bosses' money.

This highlights the biblical concept of "stewardship," which is a constant theme in the Bible. Stewardship asserts that mankind, in general, and each person, specifically, is given the opportunity to create something greater with God's resources. The time that you have on earth is temporary, and you are "loaned" some resources and are expected to use them well. In this case, the resources were the bosses' money. The principle of stewardship demands that the money be invested to create an increase.

This is, of course, an extension of the very first principle of biblical businesses. Remember, in the Garden of Eden, God gave man the Garden, as a temporary steward, to "keep and work the Garden." He leant Adam temporary authority over some aspect of creation and expected wise choices.

Not only does the principle of stewardship call on the managers to create an increase in the bosses' money but the principle also applies to the boss himself. In the way that he gave the manager's temporary authority to make decisions about his money, so too he had been given temporary authority over the business that generated that wealth and the money itself. Just as the boss will hold the managers accountable for their stewardship, so too will he be held accountable for his stewardship.

On the flip side of stewardship is another key component of biblical businesses: effective delegation. The story is just as much about the boss's delegation as it is the manager's stewardship. Note that he delegated various portions of his wealth to them, "each according to his ability."

To do that, he would need to know his employees well enough to make an informed judgment about their abilities. Once again, we are back at a consistent theme of biblical businesses: the intense relationship between the head of the business and the folks who worked in the business. But this time, we see it from the perspective of the head of the household. In this case, the owner had to know each of these managers well enough that he could distinguish their abilities and delegate to each that portion of his wealth that he thought they could handle. There was a reason why one was given five bags of gold and another just one.

How long would it have taken that business owner to develop that kind of relationship with his people? How many conversations, how many tasks assigned and completed, how many previous successful delegations? This story is not about a situation early in the relationship, but rather one that occurred after some history. It takes time to develop confidence in another person to the level that one would give them total authority over an amount this large. Five bags of gold, each the equivalent of twenty years of wages. That is one hundred years of wages, represented in those five bags. This is likely not the first time this boss delegated something to these managers.

So, we have discovered a facet in this concept of delegation: the need to know the person deeply enough to be able to accurately assess their abilities. The second part of that is to delegate tasks based on that knowledge. Each of the managers was given the task to which his abilities were sufficient. In other words, the one-bag-of-gold person did not get five bags because the boss knew his limit. The two-bag person was not given five bags for the same reason. While the boss was not happy with the results the one bag person achieved, imagine what would happen if he had given him stewardship of five bags?

Finally, a little bit of thinking uncovers another key element of delegation—appropriate risk. To have given the two-bag person control of five bags would have been too great a risk. The same is true for the one-bag person.

While it is one thing to delegate responsibility, that delegation has to occur within the greater context of the good of the entire entity. He could have given all eight bags to one person but did not. That would have been too much risk in one decision. The entire business could have been wiped out by wayward decisions. So, he chose to spread the risk among the three, with each being delegated that portion of the total store of wealth with which the boss felt most comfortable.

So, in this parable, we have uncovered the concept of stewardship and the concepts of delegation and risk, and reiterated the theme of the intense relationship between the head and the employees.

However, we have not exhausted the depth of wisdom in this story yet. Let us look at two more pieces, the first of which is reward and punishment. The two good managers, who made wise decisions and increased the master's wealth, were rewarded with yet greater responsibilities. Note that they were not rewarded with larger living quarters, a big annual bonus, better food, or better clothes. They got more responsibilities! Therefore, the biblical reward for effective stewardship is stewardship over a greater set of responsibilities and resources.

> Well done, good and faithful servant! You have been faithful with a few things; I will put you in charge of many things. Come and share your master's happiness!

At first, that might seem a bit odd. We are used to more tangible rewards. We win a trip overseas, an annual bonus, or a big commission check. But it tracks very consistently with the Bible's view of work and business. Let us go back to the Garden again. We noted that man was made in God's image, to be a worker and to be creative in his work, impacting creation with his unique perspective and talents. The reward for work done well is the opportunity to do it again on a larger scale.

Remember the Hebrew midwives? The reward for obedience—work done well—was their own businesses. In other words, it was the opportunity to do work on a larger scale. Abraham did well with his business, and the reward was a larger business—more people to impact, more of God's creation to organize and nurture.

In the biblical view, work is where God interacts with humanity. The reward for work done well is the opportunity to do more on a larger scale. In other words, it is to interact with God on a different plane. As you do work well, God invites you to a deeper level of relationship with him. Note the second part of the boss's comments to his manager: "Come and share your master's happiness!"

There are two aspects of reward for those who do well: (1) the opportunity to do it again on a larger scale and (2) a closer relationship with God. Note that the boss did not say "I'll make you happy." Rather, he said, "Share your master's happiness." Sharing implies a relationship, a spending time together. To share means that you are giving up something of yours to the other person. In this case, the boss (God) is sharing his happiness. There is a sense of doing this "happiness thing" together.

> There are two aspects of reward for those who do well: (1) the opportunity to do it again on a larger scale and (2) a closer relationship with God.

But we are not done with this parable until we look at the one-bag man.

> Then the man who had received one bag of gold came. "Master," he said, "I knew that you are a hard man, harvesting where you have not sown and gathering where you have not scattered seed. So I was afraid and went out and hid your gold in the ground. See, here is what belongs to you." His master replied, "You wicked, lazy servant! So you knew that I harvest where I have not sown and gather where I have not scattered seed? Well then, you should have put my money on deposit with the bankers, so that when I returned I would have received it back with interest. So take the bag of gold from him and give it to the one who has ten bags. For whoever has will be given more, and they will have an abundance. Whoever does not have, even what they have will be taken from them. And throw that worthless servant outside, into the darkness, where there will be weeping and gnashing of teeth." (Matt. 10:24–30)

What was the one bag's person motivation? Fear. He said, "So I was afraid." And that fear led him to do the very thing that angered his boss the most—he hid the money in the ground instead of putting it in the bank. He chose the lowest- risk option and the option that called for the minimum investment of his time and

energy. His fear led to avoidance of risk and refusal to be engaged.

There is no place in a biblical business for fear—or fear to the degree that it paralyzes one's actions and avoids all risk. In the biblical lexicon, fear of this kind is a tool of evil, used to inhibit positive actions and paralyze godly efforts. There is a passage in 2 Timothy 1:7 that puts it into perspective:

> For God did not give you a spirit of fear, but of love and power and self-control.

So, in the parable, the one-bag person allowed fear to influence him and, as a result, made the decision that required the least of him and represented the lowest-risk option.

The boss was not happy. "You could have at least put it in the bank," he declares, reflecting on an option that was low- risk yet still produced a return. But any risk was too much risk for the fearful man. His punishment tracks perfectly with the concept behind the reward the others received.

Whereas the good servants were rewarded with greater responsibilities, the worthless servant was relieved of all his responsibilities. Whereas the good servants were rewarded with greater fellowship with the boss, the worthless servant gets exactly the opposite—thrown outside where the boss doesn't live and where there is misery and sadness.

Recap

Let us recap what we can learn about biblical businesses from the teachings of Jesus:

1. Jesus viewed the household, or business, as the cellular unit of society and the economy.

2. Businesspeople have a responsibility to be good stewards of what has been entrusted to them and to invest it wisely.

3. Good businesspeople know their employees well and delegate responsibility based on their knowledge of the capabilities of the person.

4. Good businesspeople hold their employees accountable for what they have entrusted to them and reward good efforts with additional responsibilities and a closer relationship.

5. Good businesspeople provide negative consequences to those who operate out of fear and do not bring a return on their owners' investment.

Thinking about this chapter...

1. What do you make of the fact that Jesus operated on the assumption that the household was the cellular unit of society and the economy?

2. Note at least three things you can learn about biblical businesses from the parable of the bags of gold.

3. React to this statement: the reward for work done well is the opportunity to do more on a larger scale. In other words, to interact with God on a different plane. As you do work well, God invites you to a deeper level of relationship with him.

NINE

Biblical Businesses in the New Testament

As you recall, the Old Testament told the story of the creation, the ups and downs of the Jewish people, and God's relationship with them. There are sixty-six different books, written by thirty-nine authors, and I have quoted from some them.

The Old Testament writings pretty much stopped around 500 BC, and there was a period of approximately five hundred years with no scriptural record. Then the New Testament picks up with the story of Jesus and the expansion of Christianity following his resurrection. The reason it is called the New Testament is that it revolves around a new relationship between God and mankind. Now, as a result of the ministry of Jesus, everyone (not just the Jewish people) can have a relationship with God. And the Law of Moses, which contained the Ten Commandments and countless other laws, is brought to fulfillment, and a new law is instituted—the law of love that is centered around Jesus.

The story of the life, death, and resurrection of Jesus is told in the four Gospels: Matthew, Mark, Luke, and John, named for the authors of each work. The Acts of the Apostles chronicles the expansion of the Christian movement, and the epistles, which are letters written by various apostles to the Christian communities around the world, add depth and detail to the question of how to live like a Christian. The final book in the Bible, the book of Revelation, records a vision from the apostle John and articulates, in very symbolic language, the end of the world.

There are lots of differences between them. The Old Testament, for example, was written in Hebrew and authored for the Jewish people. The New Testament was primarily written in Greek and written for the world.

We are not interested, in this book, in the similarities and differences. This is a business book, not a theological discussion. However, it is helpful to gain a little background. The passages in the previous chapter in which we quoted the words of Jesus were all contained in the New Testament. There are, however, some other things about biblical businesses that we can glean from the New Testament writings in much the same way as we did the Old Testament. Other than the teachings of Jesus, discussed in the previous chapter, we learn about biblical business by seeing them in operation rather than learning from specific directions. There are few "Thou shalt do this" in the New Testament when it comes to businesses. With that as background, let us see what we can learn about biblical businesses from the New Testament.

They sometimes were large enough to have layers of management.

> Joanna the wife of Chuza, the manager of Herods *household.* (Luke 8:3, italics added)

Yes, that is the same Herod who was instrumental in Jesus's death. He had a household, the business of which was governing the territory. Evidently, his household was large enough to have middle managers, and this passage notes that the wife of Herod's CEO had converted to Christianity. A little touch of irony.

Businesses were an integral part of the training ground for the development of Christian leadership.

> A deacon must be faithful to his wife and must manage his children and his *household* well. (1 Tim. 3:12, italics added)

As Christianity began to expand, communities of Christians began to organize. The writing of the apostles identified some works of service that were somewhat specialized and focused on the evolving groups of Christians. One such work of service was that of a "deacon."

Note that the deacon gained his experience and wisdom in dealing with people through the interactions within his family and his business. Businesses, in the New Testament times, were the proving ground for the development of the qualities of character that were effective in Christian communities. Christian servants must shape their abilities in the caldron of a business.

The head of the household was expected to provide a living for all the members of that household:

> Anyone who does not provide for their relatives, and especially for their own household, has denied the faith and is worse than an unbeliever. (1 Tim. 5:8)

This passage underscores our observation that the fundamental purpose of the household, from mankind's perspective, was the physical survival of its members. If, from God's perspective, there was an additional, higher purpose of a business to provide a venue for a relationship with Him, a place to develop faith and shape character, then those who don't work deny themselves the opportunity to interact with God. This is so basic that it is a test of fellowship for the Christian CEO.

The spiritual significance of the business expands

In the Old Testament, we noted that businesses took on spiritual significance. In the beginning, God created work— and by extension, business—as the venue in which he would interact with humanity. We saw that the command to be circumcised was left in the hands of the business people. We saw that business and the marketplace were the places where spiritual gifts were exercised. In addition, we saw that God chose businesspeople to lead almost every major movement of His people.

All these point to a spiritual significance for the biblical business. In the New Testament, that spiritual significance is given a figurative shot of steroids.

The spread of Christianity in the early days was, to a large degree, achieved through the conversion of households— everyone at the same time.

The church was born on the holy day of Pentecost after Christ's resurrection with a major event in Jerusalem. The Bible indicates that over three thousand Jews were converted and baptized in that first day. After a period of solidification, the church was ready for the next step: going off into the world and making disciples of every nation.

It was at this point that the primacy of business in God's strategy became apparent. He used the business— which was already an entity that provided physical sustenance, prosperity, a sense of identity, and a set of relationships—as the cellular unit of the infant church.

First, we witness a phenomenon that set the stage for the pattern that continued through the early days of the Church— the head of the business believing and the whole organization then following that lead. God worked through businesses to achieve his purpose.

We can pick up the story in the book of Acts. The apostles were active in and around Jerusalem, preaching the good news of Jesus to the Jewish people. They viewed the ministry of Jesus as an extension of the way God had worked with the Jewish people. It never occurred to them the good news was to be shared with non-Jewish people, known as the gentiles. However, God had other plans, and He signaled his intentions via a prophecy. Here is the story. As Peter was traveling, he stopped at an inn to get something to eat and rest a bit. There, he fell into a trance and saw a vision. As he is pondering the meaning of it, some other visitors arrive. They are emissaries from Cornelius, a Roman centurion who lived in the area. Before this, Peter and all the Jewish apostles would have been extremely reluctant to speak to a gentile, especially a Roman military commander. But Peter then understood his vision as directing him to take the gospel to the Gentiles as well as the Jews. So, he went with Cornelius's servants to visit in the home of the Roman commander and to share the good news with him. This was a major turning point in the spread of Christianity as now the gospel was available to the Gentiles as well as the Jews.

Peter shares the good news with Cornelius, and he and his whole household convert. Later, Peter tells the story to the other apostles in Jerusalem. He notes that he was visited by an angel, who had said to Cornelius,

He [Peter] will bring you a message through which you and all your *household* will be saved. (Acts 11:14, italics added)

So, this major shift in the development of Christianity was accomplished in the household of a Roman centurion! And in a pattern that is later to be repeated over and over again, we witness a phenomenon: the CEO of the business converting to Christ and the entire organization then following his lead. We can only speculate on the reasons that, for this major movement of God, he chose the head of a biblical business to pave the way. This is, of course, in complete harmony with the way in which God accomplished the major movements in his plan— choosing a businessperson to lead almost every major movement.

Here is the next instance. The Apostle Paul and his companion, Silas, were traveling to Philippi, the leading city in the district of Macedonia. There they met Lydia, a businesswoman whose business was dealing in purple cloth. At the time, that was a very expensive product, purchased by the rich and the royal. Lydia was probably an upper-class businessperson. Paul taught her about Jesus, and she and her whole business became Christians.

> When she and the members of her *household* were baptized, she invited us to her home. "If you consider me a believer in the Lord," she said, "come and stay at my house." And she persuaded us. (Acts 16:15, italics added)

Here's another instance of that same pattern. Paul and Silas are arrested, beaten, and thrown into prison. About midnight, there is a miraculous earthquake, all the prison doors fly open, and everyone's chains are unlocked. The jailer wakes up, sees the state of things, and prepared to kill himself because he knows he will be held accountable for the prisoners. Paul stops him and tells him about Jesus.

> At that hour of the night the jailer took them and washed their wounds; then immediately he and all his *household* were baptized. (Acts 16:33, italics added)

And there it is again. The pattern repeats itself. The CEO converts to Christianity, and the entire organization follows. Here is yet another example. When it came time to penetrate the city of Corinth with the gospel, again the target was a business. It was not just any business but that of Crispus, the synagogue leader. I cannot imagine a more significant household to lead the way.

> Crispus, the synagogue leader, and his entire *household* believed in the Lord; and many of the Corinthians

who heard Paul believed and were baptized. (Acts 18:8, italics added)

I will spare you additional examples, as I think I have made my point. You get the sense from these verses that when a head of the household converted to Christianity, because of the relationships previously developed, the entire household followed the lead of its head. In the examples cited above, these existing organizations of people—united in relationships, common purpose, and physical proximity— converted en masse.

The biblical business truly had spiritual significance in the New Testament.

Following their conversion, biblical businesses provided the nucleus of the emerging church.

But that's not all. As Christianity moved throughout the known world, small communities of new Christians popped up all over. Following the act of conversion, they began to meet together to learn from and assist one another. Frequently, the business provided the venue, the infrastructure, and the relationships that made these communities effective. In other words, as the household worked together to expand its own prosperity, it offered an environment where people worked together, got to know each other, and created relationships with one another. No need to find a place to meet—they were already meeting at the business location. No need to create leaders—they were already there. No need to create new relationships—they were already in place. As an organization of people, the biblical business was already in place and functioning. Now, the business began to function as a church as well as a business.

> Greet Priscilla and Aquila, my fellow workers in Christ Jesus. Greet also the church that meets at their house. (Rom. 16:3, 5)

This church met in the house of Priscilla and Aquila. The house was where most, if not all, of the household, lived. Was this church made up of members of their business? It most likely was.

In the following passages, note how the Apostle Paul refers to groups of believers in the context of their household or business.

> Greet those who belong to the household of Aristobulus. (Rom. 16:10)

> My brothers, some from Chloe's household have informed me that there are quarrels among you. (1 Cor. 1:11)

> You know that the household of Stephanas were the first converts in Achaia, and they have devoted themselves to the service of the saints. (1 Cor. 16:15)

While we do not have a verse that says, "This business morphed into a church," you do get a sense from the passages noted above that is exactly what happened.

God was active in businesses in the New Testament stories.

What does this have to do with you?

So what? What does that have to do with your business or your future business today? Not every business converted to Christianity en masse, and not every business became the nucleus of an emerging church. However, many did.

This view of a biblical business is not for everyone. However, there may be some of you who want to use their businesses to create a more lasting impact than just making money. You may seek a greater degree of fulfillment and purpose in your life. If so, the place to look is within the biblical business. There is a potential, at least for some, to move beyond just making money and providing economic security for folks to becoming spiritual juggernauts.

While we are on the subject of what the New Testament has to say about businesses, it is worthwhile to note one more interesting element.

God speaks of his people as being members of his business.

The common practice among people interested in the Bible in today's culture is to read the word translated as "household" in many contemporary translations and assume it means "family." While that feels good, it is not accurate. As we have seen, households are larger than families, and they have servants, slaves, employees, and layers of management. A more accurate understanding of "households" is "businesses." We have made that point earlier in this book.

Before we look at these passages, I felt it appropriate to revisit that issue. Remember, when we first encounter God, he is working. Now, we understand that he has an enterprise, a business in the same sense that we have used the term throughout the manuscript: There is a work to be done, and a group of folks, headed by an individual, are organized to do that work.

Here is a way to look at it. God's family consists of one Son, Jesus, and a relative, the Holy Spirit. But his household consists of that family and all the angels aligned with his purpose. And that is not all. As human beings encounter God, some commit to following Jesus. They are then "adopted sons" of God and become part of his household. Let us see what the New Testament has to say about that:

> Consequently, you are no longer foreigners and strangers, but fellow citizens with God's people and also members of his *household*. (Eph. 2:19, italics added)

> If I am delayed, you will know how people ought to conduct themselves in God's *household*, which is the church of the living God, the pillar and foundation of the truth. (1 Tim. 3:15, italics added)

> For it is time for judgment to begin with God's *household*; and if it begins with us, what will the outcome be for those who do not obey the gospel of God? (1 Pet. 4:17, italics added)

While there is a lot of discussion that can be had

around these notions, let us leave that for a religious book. For our purposes, notice how important businesses are to God. In his view, the cellular organizational unit is not the family, not the local church, and not the city. It is the household—the biblical business.

> If you are a business person, you should be awed by the incredible spiritual potential that exists within your business.

Thinking about this chapter...

1. Compare and contrast the biblical mandate that "deacons" should prove themselves in their businesses with today's practice of substituting "knowledge gained in seminaries" for wisdom gained in a business as the qualifier for Christian leadership.

2. What do you make of the fact that in the early days of the establishment of Christianity, entire businesses converted at one time?

3. What are some of the advantages of businesses morphing into churches?

Biblical Business Profile:
Performance Systematix, Inc.

Performance Systematix, Inc. is a manufacturer of packing solutions that utilize a high-tech venting technology. The business has been in existence for about thirty years and has seen some remarkable growth in the last decade.

Glenn, company president, works hard to implement a biblical culture within the organization. He came to that place in an unusual way. Glenn was hired as a vice president to open up a European division of the company. Shortly thereafter, he was approached by one of the employees, who delivered a memo to him, signed by the majority of the employees in the company, asking permission to pray together for the success of the European initiative. Glenn knew then that there was something special, in a spiritual sense, in that business.

Two years later, he was appointed president. In the next two and a half years, the business doubled in size. "I'm a good businessman," Glenn says, "but I'm not that good." He attributes the growth to God. "My role is to get out of God's way, to pray, and to wait on Him to move within the business." Believing that God wanted to be involved in the business, Glenn first had to invite Him in and open himself to God's involvement in the business. That meant beginning with a commitment to a personal "surrender." "I had to give up my personal ego, pray a lot, and wait on God. I had to first be willing to listen and then be willing to be obedient."

That takes a disciplined approach. Glenn begins every day in private prayer and then walks through the facility, chatting with the employees and praying for them and the business. He will often ask someone who is going through a difficult time if he can pray for him or her.

According to him, "Most of our learning, both as a business as well as in regards to our faith, comes as a result of a time of crises. My job is to come alongside of them, to remove any hint of fear and to help them grow."

This concern for the well-being of the company's employees is one of the identifying characteristics of the biblical business. It expresses itself in some tangible ways in Performance Systematics. "We have, on more than one occasion, kept someone on the payroll for a year or more when they were unable to perform their duties," Glenn says. "We constantly challenge people to grow, both spiritually and in their business acumen."

Waiting on God to work in the business and to create opportunities for spiritual and business growth has resulted in significant progress in both areas. The business is highly profitable and has no debt. Spiritually, Glenn has a sense of "the body of Christ working within this company." Every Thursday at lunchtime, for example, a group of employees meets outside of the business for a Bible study, which is open to everyone.

What is unique in Glenn's experience is the fact that he is not an owner but works for an owner who does not share the depth of Glenn's spiritual commitment. The owner has given Glenn leeway to manage the business in a biblical manner.

"It's a wise business decision for him to do so," Glenn remarked. "He gets an executive who has integrity, who treats people well—both of which are good business traits, regardless of one's spiritual inclinations."

And the business has prospered under that approach. "Doing business God's way is just good business—regardless of your spiritual motivation."

TEN

A Consolidated Picture of Biblical Businesses

In this chapter, we will pull together our observations of biblical businesses into a profile of what one looks like and then extend that to twenty-first-century businesses.

Here is what we have learned so far:

1. God created the earth as a place for man to work and chose to interact with him in that work. That places work—and, by extension, businesses—very high up on the priority list. In order of sequence, work comes first—before family, before church, before recreation, and before procreation.

2. Biblical businesses are created with a purpose. At one level, from mankind's perspective, the initial

purpose is to create economic security for all the members of the household. At another level, spiritual, businesses are the venue that God has created in which to interact with humanity. The myriad relationships, the sense of being part of something larger than oneself, the process of working together—all of these combine to create a place where the sensitive spiritual person can develop his/her spirituality and enrich his/her faith.

3. They have specific purposes given to them by God. This is the work for which the business engages— being a cleaner, a restaurant, a stockbroker, etc. In a very real sense, just as God gave Adam the task to name the animals and then chose to work with him in that task, so God gives people today their tasks— their businesses—and chooses to work with people in their businesses. In a larger sense, every biblical business has the same purpose mentioned above. In a specific sense, each business is unique and is focused on a purpose that is right for it. If you have a business, believe that it is given to you by God. If you want to have a business, ask him to give you the work upon which the business will focus.

4. They are marked by the intense relationship between the head of the business and the employees within it. This is one of the distinguishing characteristics of biblical businesses. The employees, servants, and slaves respected and honored the head of the business, who had made it his priority to know and take care of each.

5. The business is often blessed or cursed because of the actions of one of its members, particularly the head of the business. The employees and owners of a biblical business truly are in the enterprise together. If God made man to be communal and social, he also gave him the place where he could be that—the business.

6. Businesses and business people are often rewarded for their good work and obedience by an increase in worldly wealth and a larger, more significant work to do as well as a closer relationship with God.

7. Biblical businesses provide a venue for the personal development of the members. Almost all the main characters in the Bible—those whose actions have generations of impact on the greater biblical narrative—spent a significant

portion of their lives in business. This underscores the principle that God uses businesses as the primary place to develop the qualities of character he wants in us.

8. Biblical businesses provide a venue for man's creativity to be exercised. God gives mankind the basic charge of creating a higher degree of organization in his creation and then gives individuals the specific task of using their creativity to create organization within a specific section of his creation. All businesses can be seen as myriad attempts to bring our creativity to God's creation in order to create yet a higher degree of organization.

9. Biblical businesses provide a setting for the exercise of spiritual gifts. From the very beginning, throughout the Bible, spiritual gifts are given for the common good. The common good is developed in the marketplace, where people have jobs, relationships, a sense of purpose, and an opportunity to encounter God and develop themselves.

10. Biblical businesses employ certain strategies: preparation for contingencies, specialization, succession planning, delegation, and risk

management, to name a few.

11. Biblical businesses are a training ground for the next generation. Instead of the business being a means to provide the resources for the children to be educated and developed somewhere else, the children were educated and developed through their responsibilities in the business.

12. Biblical businesses often evolve from being just economic entities to becoming enterprises with spiritual significance and sometimes morph into churches.

Applications to the twenty-first century

Let us take a look at what a biblical business might look like in the twenty-first century. I am assuming, at this point, that you believe in the God of the Bible and want to bring him into your business in the full biblical sense—that you are interested in realizing the full economic and spiritual potential of a biblical business.

For those folks who want to achieve the full potential of a biblical business and strive to add the spiritual component to it, this is what a twenty-first-century biblical business would look like:

A head who is a devoted person of God.

From the beginning, the head of the biblical business had a relationship with God. The Bible presents a view that in every age and time, God had a special relationship with a group of people. In the Old Testament, it was the Hebrews; and in the New, it was the disciples of Christ. Regardless, the first aspect of a biblical business today is that the head— the entrepreneur, owner, or CEO—has a relationship with God. Ultimately, the Bible story is about God seeking a relationship with mankind in general and individuals specifically. You cannot have a spiritual entity if you are outside of that spiritual relationship.

A work that fits the head's set of gifts and passions and conveys a sense that it was specifically given by God.

There are an incalculable number of works on which a biblical business can focus. Once you understand the concept of spiritual gifts, you can see that God uses his gifting of abilities and interests to, at least in part, organize the world of work. The head of a biblical business has an understanding that the work his business does is good work, given to him by God. Managing a biblical business becomes, then, a "ministry" of the highest level, with the potential to impact people's lives in this life and the next. That understanding of the spiritual impact of a biblical business allows him/her an opportunity to use the spiritual gifts and natural abilities that have been given to him.

This gives every biblical business a sense of the

nobleness of their work as well as a connection to something larger and bigger than just their day-to-day labor.

A clear understanding of the business's purposes and boundaries.

The business exists, at least on one level, to make money. Its venue is the marketplace, and it is sustainable by the income it receives for the work it does.

Also, the business has a clear, and articulate understanding of its purpose and its boundaries - where it will excel and what it will not do. This will probably take the form of a written set of vision, mission, and values statements, or a comparable written document. Those documents and the positions they articulate are routinely and systematically shared with all the stakeholders in the business.

An intense relationship between the head and the employees.

This is one of those critical elements that put biblical businesses in a different league than the normal family business. You will probably never get to the point where you can announce that all your male employees are going to be circumcised, but that is the standard to which to strive.

The intensity of the relationship implies that the

head knows each employee and his/her family. The head probably shows up at that family's graduations, weddings, and funerals, and has eaten dinner at their houses, and had them for dinner at his/hers.

The head of the biblical business has proven his/her business acumen and spiritual commitment, has proven that he/she operates out of a higher set of standards, and thereby is admired, respected, and followed by the people who work in that business.

A sense of responsibility for the well-being of the employees.

The head of a biblical business recognizes that his/her employees are gifts to him, lent to him temporarily by God, and thus accepts the responsibility to bless and care for the employees. While every business does this to some degree, a biblical business takes it to a higher level.

A family who sees themselves as an integral part of the business.

Not every head of a biblical business needs to have a family; reflect on Abraham, for example. When there is a family involved, there is, within the biblical business, a different attitude about the business in the family and a different attitude about the family in the business.

The family does not view the business as a

competitor for the head's time but rather as an extension of the family's sphere of influence and responsibility. It is not that the head goes to work; it is that the family assumes responsibility for the work and assists in any way that it can. This can mean that the spouse helps out and that all the kids have roles to play, and there may even be a spot for parents, in-laws, and siblings.

The folks in the business do not consider the owner's family to be a burden or a competition for responsibility and income. Rather, they have a sense that "we are in this together" and extend that attitude toward their own family as well.

A commitment to being guided by biblical principles and values.

Understanding that the business is a gift from God and a venue for God to interact with humans, the head is committed to doing good work and is doing it in ways that track with biblical concepts and values. For example, the business, as it grows, will incorporate the principles of specialization and preparation for contingencies and will deal ethically and honestly with all the stakeholders.

Once everyone understands that the business is involved in something bigger and more impactful than just making money, taking shortcuts and engaging in unscrupulous tactics to make money just do not appear like viable options.

A commitment to being guided by the Holy Spirit.

It is one thing to be guided by biblical principles. It is another to be guided by the Holy Spirit. There is a natural progression in the spiritual growth of an individual and, by extension, the business run by that individual. At the stage where one is guided solely by biblical principles, the responsibility for decisions remains with the individual as he/she attempts to bring biblical principles into the business. It is a higher state of spiritual awareness when the manager recognizes that the business is God's and that he/ she is the temporary steward of it. Decision-making becomes, then, a process of asking for God's direction. What would he want you to do?

The business is exactly what God designed it to be from the moment of creation—a place where he interacts with mankind, an outpost of the kingdom penetrating the lives of the employees and the industries and vendors it serves with a living, realistic picture of the providence and grace of God.

Practically, this means that the owner and those who chose to join him are in regular prayer for the business and all its stakeholders and regularly seek to hear from God. They are sensitive to not only God's responses to their inquiries but also to his proactive leading in both the day to day as well as the general direction of the business.

An understanding of biblical rewards and punishments.

Clearly, the God of the Bible blessed those households who pursued his will and obeyed him and punished those who transgressed. The twenty-first-century biblical business shares that expectation of blessing—an expectation that if they do work well and seek to continually know and obey God's directive, they will receive additional wealth and responsibilities. On the other side of the coin, they live with a healthy fear of the Lord, understanding that their deliberate transgressions are likely to result in adversity and failure.

An understanding of the potential spiritual impact of the business on family, employees, customers, vendors, and other stakeholders.

The head and, to a lesser degree, all the employees have a sense of the potential spiritual impact of the business on the folks with whom they interact. The business is, first, a means by which people are economically advantaged. In addition, there is the potential that in the relationships that are forged and the labor that is done, God will show up in some way and touch and influence folks. Thus, the business is exactly what God designed it to be from the moment of creation—a place where he interacts with mankind, an outpost of the kingdom penetrating the lives of the employees, the industries, vendors and customers it serves with a living, realistic picture of the providence and grace of God.

What if we really believed that the household or its modern version, the biblical business, was the primary unit in God's Kingdom? What if we taught that from the pulpits and in our schools?

Suppose we began to see a Christianity that acknowledged the biblical business as the nucleus of the universal church, as the vanguard for God's strategy to convert the world, and as the forefront of his plan to take back creation? If Christian businesses began to see themselves as this special light and biblical business owners began to sprout up all over the world, what would be different?

Here is a beginning list:

1. Owners of Christian businesses would see themselves as responsible for the physical and spiritual health of their employees to a much greater extent than is typically the case.

2. Owners of Christian businesses would see themselves as the "shepherds" of their households, knowing each person closely enough to be able to minister to them when necessary. In those

businesses that have grown beyond the owner's ability to personally shepherd them, he would see to it that workplace chaplains/ shepherds/pastors would fill in for him.

3. Everyone would have a much larger view of the Kingdom than just that proclaimed from the pulpits of the institutional church. Not only would the Kingdom be perceived as a spiritual entity but it would additionally be seen as operating in the physical and economic realms, providing jobs and opportunities for people, and creating wealth for all its components: owners, nuclear family, extended family, employees, customers, and stakeholders of all sorts.

4. Owning and developing a Christian business would be seen as a unique and powerful ministry. It is there where people can be discipled, where the one-anothers would best be activated, where the wealth created would enrich the lives of all the employees and provide funds for helping the poor.

5. As Christian businesses came out from under the spirit-hindering paradigms that have kept them thinking of themselves in purely worldly

terms, they would begin to see themselves as venues for the use of spiritual gifts and places and circumstances in which God shows up and does his work.

6. Christian businesses would begin to pop up more rapidly all over the planet, bringing their message of economic enhancement, personal ministry, and spiritual development with them to communities in every nation.

7. Christian businesspeople, empowered by the teaching in the parable of the bags of gold, would stop thinking of their profits as something to be given to support the religious establishment and instead would continue to reinvest those profits in the continual growth of their businesses.

8. As the economic power of the Christian businesses grew, their political influence would follow. The Christian influence on political powers would grow to be the dominant force.

9. The gospel would be proclaimed in every nation, and the Kingdom would spread wherever a biblical business could operate.

> By unleashing the entrepreneurial spirit in the economy, the Spirit would eventually penetrate every industry and, therefore, every economic class and ethnic group. The world would be converted, first by an opportunity for economic security and community offered by employment in a biblical business, and then by immersion into a lifestyle of devotion to Jesus Christ that surrounded them in that environment.

This, I believe, is a core element in God's strategy for redeeming the world.

Thinking about this chapter...

1. Of the list of things we have learned about biblical businesses, which resonates with you the most?

2. When applied to today's world, which of the characteristics most appeals to you? Why?

3. When we consider the implications of a rapid expansion of biblical businesses, which of those listed most resonates with you? Why?

4. What other implication can you see of the rapid expansion of biblical businesses?

ELEVEN

Transforming Your Business

You may have decided that you want your business to be more than just a money-making enterprise, and the biblical business model appeals to you. How do you go about transforming your business into a force for the Kingdom?

Keeping in mind the characteristics of a biblical business from the previous chapter, here's a set of recommendations for specific initiatives to pursue. Most of these are ongoing efforts which you place in your business intentionally and then continue to practice with discipline.

I. Establish prayer disciplines.

Remember that God wants to relate to you in your work and your business. You need to invite him to participate, not just once, but on a regular, disciplined basis. And the way you do that is through a robust and growing prayer life. Prayer, then, should be a regular part of your business routines.

It begins with personal prayer. Many business people find that a morning devotional of Bible reading and personal prayer is a powerful way to start the day. Some, who seek a more intense relationship with God, have used the prayer wheel. (www..christianchallenge.us/spfoPrayer-onehour.html) This results in an hour-long interaction with God. You can start once a week, and add additional sessions as you go.

At the same time that you establish personal prayer disciplines, consider building prayer routines into your business. Many Christian business people begin the week with a Monday morning prayer time with you leading and including anyone from the organization who wants to take part. Some extend that to every morning.

Still, others offer a weekly prayer time, to which all the employees are invited, but no one is coerced. Consider developing the habit of praying for and with those employees who need or ask for it. Glenn, from Performance Systematix, Inc., has created the habit of walking through the building every day, chatting with the employees, and often asking if there is something for which he can pray on their behalf. Duncan at Howell Pipe Supply maintains a 3 X 5 card for each employee, and regularly prays for them. Many Christian business people start every meeting and every company-sponsored event with a prayer.

A number of CEOs maintain a prayer team, consisting of people who have been recruited to pray for the business. Daron, at VFP, has had such a prayer team for years. I maintain a small group of prayer warriors, each of whom prays for the business on a different day of the week. One on Monday, another on Tuesday, etc. Every Saturday morning I email a list of the issues on which I'm working, upcoming challenges, and my schedule.

Still, one other option is to hire an intercessor for the business. This is someone who is particularly skilled in prayer disciplines, perhaps even gifted in it, who will come to know the business well and intercede on your behalf on a methodical and regular schedule. For years, I have had such a person who has been either a paid employee or a contractor.

The goal is to bring God into the business and into the lives of the employees in a regular, real and intense way.

2. Craft the foundational documents.

If you are going to be a business which honors God and respects his ownership of the business, it is helpful to say that in the organization's vision, mission and values statements. There is a power to verbalizing that relationship and your commitment in writing, and then posting it for all your employees, vendors and stakeholders to see.

Once you say it, and then write it down, you are committed to a higher degree then if you don't write it down. The act of writing forces a precision and allows you the opportunity to review and edit until you get it right. As an example, on the next page are the documents I created in 1994.

3. Gather a group of advisors

Understand the wisdom from Proverbs 15:22 (NASBRE):

> Plans fail when there is no counsel, but they succeed when **advisers** are many.

This passage is not just a wise thought, but a specific piece of guidance for every head of a business. As a consultant for 25 + years, I can tell you that almost every business person is too close to the details of his/her business to have a clear view of the bigger picture. What is glaringly obvious to an outsider is often obscure to those inside the business. If you are going to build a powerful organization, you'll need to make sure that you avoid the pitfalls and focus on the appropriate challenges and opportunities. And that means gathering a group of trusted advisers around you.

At one end of the spectrum of possibilities, you

could have a small group of paid advisers who meet together with you on a regular (quarterly or monthly) schedule. If that is too expensive, you may consider one of the CEO Roundtable groups: C-12, Convene, or Truth@Work (with whom I am associated):

VISION & VALUES

To continually increase our positive impact on people and organizations while remaining in the center of God's direction and reflecting His character.

Profit: We will earn a better than average profit as this allows us the flexibility to do other things.

Integrity: We will be honest in everything we do, never over promise, and zealously work to fulfill our commitments.

Open-minded: We will constantly be open to new or different ideas, methods and concepts from all sources, especially our clients.

Learning: We will value individual and organizational learning (the ability to continually take in new information, acquire new insights, and change in positive ways as a result of that information) as our primary competitive advantage.

Humility: We will constantly be aware that the resources we use and the clients we serve are gifts from God, entrusted to our temporary stewardship.

Quality: In everything we do, we will strive to do it as well as, or better than, the very best companies in the world like ours do it.

Regardless of how organized our effort is, keep in mind that that the purpose is to create a committed group of advisers, who have a degree of outside expertise, and who are on your side, holding you accountable for your business success.

4. Include your family in the business

Remember, the biblical response to work-family balance is to bring your family into the business. This may require thoughtful intentionality on your part. It could range from sharing your day with your spouse over the dinner table, to finding employment from your kids, siblings, and in-laws. Working together on the family business brings you together, gives you a common higher purpose, provides a topic of conversation, and gets everyone contributing to the same end.

Many Christian business people employ their spouses and their kids. Every one of my children, as they were growing up, had work to do in the business. Sometimes it was an hour a week or so on a project, and other times it was full-time employment. In my days as a sales person, I would take each of the kids, by himself/herself, for a day with me during the summer. They would dress up and go into every sales call with me. We'd have lunch together, and talk about how each call went. It is a fond memory for all of us.

5. Intentionally work at crafting a culture.

Corporate culture develops over time, and all too often by chance. You have an opportunity to craft your culture by design. Give some thought to what you want to create and intentionally begin to find stories and examples that illustrate those. As you come across an event or a story that illustrates an aspect of the culture you want, repeat the story and emphasize the lesson it teaches.

There is a copious quantity of wisdom and information out there on corporate culture, and how to create a culture that reflects your values. Take it seriously and dig into it

A key part of a biblical business culture is the incredibly close relationship between the head and other members of the organization. This takes work on your part. It could begin with keeping track of each employee, like Duncan does, walking around and praying for them, like Glenn, or investing time and energy in one, like Daron. (See the Biblical Business Profiles in this book) It certainly would involve intentionally seeking to know each employee better, to be a larger part of his/her life by attending weddings, funerals, and graduations.

Your goal is to create such a strong relationship with your team that they will respect and follow you almost anywhere you want to go.

6. Get continuously better at your business.

Continuous improvement, for a Biblical business, is not an option. You need to do good work. And the definition of that, in today's rapidly changing economy, continuously changes.

That means, from a very practical perspective, that you need to continuously improve your product or service, your systems and your technology and tools to stay current or ahead of the mass of the market. This requires a commitment from you and an active openness to seek the next best thing for your offerings.

7. Be sensitive to opportunities to grow in size and influence.

Understand that the Biblical reward for being obedient and doing business well is greater responsibility and a closer relationship with God. That generally means a bigger business.

The more customers, employees, vendors and stakeholders you have, the more influence you have. The more influence you have, the greater the opportunity to channel God's grace, economic security and spiritual connections.

Put in place some processes and procedures to recognize opportunities for growth which come your way. If God wants to bless your obedience and good work with a larger opportunity and more customers, you don't want to miss it because you weren't expecting it.

8. *Encourage others to add to the movement.*

One way to give back and to spread your influence is to actively seek opportunities to mentor and encourage others. As you raise people up, consider releasing them to an opportunity to develop their own biblical business (Innogroup companies provides an excellent model).

Presenting at colleges and high schools, nurturing interns, sharing your views with others at association and industry meetings all are ways to spread the word. You never know who in your audience may turn into a Biblical business entrepreneur.

If you want to dig into these practices more intensely, review the Biblical Business Course here: https://www.thebiblicalbusiness.com/biblical-business-coalition/

Thinking about this chapter...

1. Which of the prayer disciplines described could you see yourself implementing soon in your business?

2. What are the advantages and disadvantages of committing yourself to be a Kingdom business on paper, in your vision, mission and values statement?

3. How do you see yourself gathering a group of advisers?

4. What, specifically, could you do to bring your family into the business?

5. What practices could you engage in that what build an organizational culture?

6. What could you do to improve continuously?

7. How could you be sensitive to opportunities to grow your business size and influence?

8. How could you encourage others to add to the movement?

TWELVE

Implications for Families

Much is said these days about the family as the cellular unit of societal organization. In the Bible, though, the family is not nearly as predominant as the business!

The idea that our families are our highest earthly priority is one of those paradigms that are universally accepted. Who could argue with that? We hear people say, "God first, family second." Our children have become the focus of our lives, and our lives revolve around them. Pictures of them and stories about them overwhelm our social media. Many people even substitute pictures of their children for themselves on their social media profiles. We schedule soccer practice, musical practices, and a myriad of other activities designed to help them reach their potential. Parents cart them from one event o another to such a degree that the situation has spawned the term 'soccer mom.'

Many parents accept the idea that they need to provide a college education for them, and that need dictates many decisions in their lives. The mantra of "God first, family second" is the subject of sermons from the pulpit and conversations around the water cooler. Who could question it?

Before we go any deeper into the issue, it is helpful to be reminded of a core principle: the Bible makes it clear that God does not think the way we do. That principle is a bedrock principle to understanding the Bible and crops up all over the place. Probably the clearest conveyance of that idea is contained in the book of Isaiah.

Isaiah was a prophet who, among other things, predicted the coming of the Messiah, Jesus Christ. Prophets were a special group of people who appeared from time to time in the Hebrew history and who claimed a special ability to hear directly from God. Their writings are full of comments that attribute the words in them directly to God.

The passage below is just one of a multiple number that make the same claim:

'For my thoughts are not your thoughts, neither are your ways my ways,' declares the Lord. (Isa. 55:8)

In other words, it is likely that in many things, what we think are good and proper are not what God thinks. There is often a difference between what man believes and values and what the Bible reveals about what God values.

Could that be a part of our understanding of the importance of families?

When the Bible speaks of families, it almost always uses the term in reference to the bloodline. There is an example in this record of the scheming of Lot's daughters. You remember the story of Sodom and Gomorrah, two cities destroyed by God for their wickedness. Lot and his two daughters, aided by angels, escape the destruction and then hide in a cave. Life is dull and lonely for Lot's daughters, who, despairing of finding a husband, decide on a different path to having children. The Bible records the conversation:

> Let's get our father to drink wine and then sleep with him and preserve our *family* line through our father. (Gen. 19:32, italics added)

While there is a lot to talk about in this verse, the thing that is pertinent to our discussion is the use of "family" to signify the bloodline.

When the Bible refers to what we call the extended family, the word "household" is used. As we have seen, the household is a larger unit, comprised of family, servants, slaves, and employees. The household is a business, not a family.

So, the Bible rarely speaks about families, in our sense of the word. Rather, the Bible speaks of households. Remember, a household is a much larger group—a business—consisting of the nuclear family, the extended family, and the servants, slaves, and employees associated with the business.

Add it all up, and it should be clear that it is the household—the family business—that is the cellular unit of society in the biblical perspective. Nuclear families, as we like to think of them, were not nearly as important to God as the household.

I realize that is a difficult concept for a lot of us to get our heads around. We hear the message of "family first" from all kinds of sources, over and over again. Could it be that the Bible actually presents a concept of business first?

Is there any indication, anywhere in the Bible, that the head of the household had any greater responsibility to his children than he did to his servants and employees?

Let us just suspend our preconceived notions a moment and consider the implications. What if we changed our thinking and, instead of thinking about our family, began to think regarding our businesses?

In Western society, the children often become the focus of the energies of the parents and grandparents. What if the survival and prosperity of the household were of higher value and the children were seen as having a responsibility to contribute to that purpose? Would our children grow up to be more responsible, more sensitive to others, and more realistically aware of their place in the world?

One of the most poignant conflicts that afflict us is the challenge to balance time between family and the job. This is particularly true of small business owners. They could easily put in twenty-four hours a day in the business. Yet every hour spent in the business is an hour spent away from the family—a case made passionately by their spouses and families. On the other hand, the business will not survive and prosper without the owner's hands-on tending to it. So, much of the small business owner's life is spent managing a fundamental conflict.

There is not a businessperson who has not felt that conflict. Multiple books have been written on the subject, and blog posts with solutions abound. It is hard not to feel guilty about the demands that the business puts on them. It seems like they either deprive their family of precious time or they rob the business of their input.

But what if we have this wrong? What if the solution were both, not either-or? I believe that is exactly the situation that the biblical household offers. Remember, a household is a conglomeration of people often, but not always, centered around the core family, who are involved in some business. They manage and create wealth for the household with the goal of providing prosperity for everyone involved, not just for today but also for generations to come. Biblical businesses are the venue for God to interact with His people, for faith to be developed, and for character to be shaped. And isn't that what we want for our children? If we could pull that off, wouldn't we be great parents?

The household provided the opportunity for the family to be engaged together in a joint pursuit. In other words, the business was not divorced from the family but was something the family did together. They were intimately intertwined.

Conventional wisdom urges us to allocate our time between our family and our business. The Bible knows of no such distinction. The biblical approach is to bring your family into the business!

> Instead of allocating your time between your family and your business, be guided by the biblical example and bring your family into the business.

Now imagine what our society would be like if we could multiply the number of biblical businesses by a factor of ten. There would be an immediate impact on families and on the greater society as a whole. The sense of entitlement that we see as a characteristic of those entering the workforce today would be eliminated, at least in biblical business families. Children would respect work and understand their responsibility to contribute to the well-being of the business. The teenage problems of out-of-wedlock pregnancies, alcohol and substance abuse and irresponsible behavior would all be lessened by the impact of biblical businesses.

If we were to multiply the number of biblical businesses and change the attitude toward them, we would go a long way to solving the family problems that are epidemic in this country.

Thinking about this chapter...

1. To what degree do you agree with the assertion that modern society holds families first, but the biblical patterns hold businesses up as a higher priority?

2. If we were to wave a magic wand and create ten times as many biblical businesses, how would families in this society be impacted?

3. To what degree does the current view of "families first, businesses are unimportant" enlarge the position of the religious establishment and degrade the position of biblical businesses?

Biblical Business Profile:
Home Coders

Home Coders is Josh Roley's company in which he finds software developers who want to work from home, and matches them to employers who hire them. Sometimes the employer hires the developer, and Josh makes a percentage of the transaction, and other times they work with the developer on a contract-to-hire basis. Using Malachi 4:6 as his focus, Josh feels that he is doing good work as well as providing a good income for his household. This start-up business takes about half of Josh's time and provides more than half of his income.

A second income stream comes from his work as a home- based salesperson for a business run by one of his friends. This company sells reciprocating pumps to a national market over the Web and via phone. Josh works from his home office as a contractor to this business, and it provides almost half of his income and a little less than half of his time.

He additionally has a small income stream from

commission sales work for a former employer. He spends one or two days a month nurturing relationships he created in his previous job, and it provides a small percentage of his income. The final stream of income comes from projects the family creates that intentionally involve Josh's children. He has six children, ages five months through eleven, and is committed to developing an entrepreneurial spirit in them. The family raised dogs, for example, with each of the older children making the decision to invest fifty dollars into a stud fee. They each netted $350 out of the project and had responsibilities to help care for the animals. The family has paid some Amish neighbors to raise grass-fed cattle and then sells them by the quarter. The next step in this project is to raise a steer or two on their own.

This combination of home and family-based income streams provide the family with an annual income of six figures.

Developing economic sense in his children is something about which Josh and Shane, his wife, are passionate. Each child has a bank account and is guided in making investments that bring them a potential return. The dog breeding business is one such example, as is the grass-fed cattle. This year, the kids are creating a vegetable garden, and the family will buy the vegetables from them at market rates.

Josh has a vision that his children will be able to buy their own homes, for cash with no debt, by the time each is married. "Home" has a big part of Josh's vision in how to live a Christian life in these times. Both he and Shane were good church kids growing up, attending public schools and a Christian college. It was a pretty conventional upbringing. He recounts how the Lord moved him to this position via his wife's illness. Just prior to their marriage, Shane was diagnosed with a life-threatening connective tissue disease. The prognosis of the medical doctors was twenty years of medication, sterility, and an early death. She did some research and decided to radically change her diet; and within six months, she was healed.

If the conventional wisdom was so far away from the truth in this instance, they reasoned, what about other areas of life? What another blessing might they be missing by mindlessly buying into the world's systems and paradigms?

Armed with a quest to find God's truth for their lives, Josh and Shane have realized that "there is something terribly broken in the way Christians are living today."

They have arrived at:
- A home-based business for Josh,
- Homeschooling for the kids, and
- Home church for the family.

Josh reflects on the intimate involvement God has had in their lives and the role his decisions have made on building the family's faith. To have six children, for example, takes a growing faith in God and the willingness to trust him. "You need a big God on your side to provide for us," Josh reflects. He tells how the Lord has guided them along the way. One dramatic instance occurred as Shane wanted to move near her family. After a time of prayer and seeking the Lord's will, they felt the Lord was directing them to move to Deerfield. Wanting to be obedient, they put their house up for sale, Josh gave notice to his employer, and the family started looking for a home in Deerfield, Michigan, near Shane's parents. Door after door closed in their attempt to move, and eventually, they gave up, thinking that maybe they had misunderstood the Lord's leading.

A year later, they were led to purchase the home they now have, in Deerfield Township. They had no idea there was a Deerfield Township in West Michigan. In the fall of 2008, in the midst of the housing crises, they sold their home in seven days and bought their current home—three acres, four thousand square feet, a perfect home to raise six children, and in the midst of Amish country.

"You can't plan your way into God's favor and grace," Josh says.

Josh and Shane are continuous learners. Josh is

constantly reading books, listening to podcasts, and interacting with Web sites to enhance his skills and business concepts as well as to expand his view of how the Lord works in the household's life. Josh had a mentor for about a year and was a member of a Truth@Work Christian Executive Roundtable, where he was surrounded by Christian businesspeople who held him accountable and provided a support group. Josh recounts how he took a business opportunity to the group and the assembled wisdom was not to pursue it. Josh credits that advice with saving him thousands of dollars and lots of headaches.

An interesting adjunct to Joshs efforts to build a God- honoring household is the familys involvement in a house church. Four families meet together, often in Josh's home.

As is typical of home churches, there are no positions, no programs, and no doctrinal statements. The families meet, have a meal together, pray, sing, and share in a free-flowing, unscripted gathering that approximates Paul's teaching in 1 Corinthian 14:26. Their focus is to "spur one another on toward love and good works" (Heb. 10:24).

THIRTEEN

Biblical Businesses, You, The Economy, and The Culture

What would your own personal economic situation look like if you were to develop a Christian family business along the lines of the biblical household? What would the national economy look like if biblical businesses were to proliferate? Let us think about each of these in the order in which we have them noted. What would it look like if you were to have a Christian business?

It would be, first of all, Christian. That means that you would, first of all, have a relationship with Christ and that you would be firmly grounded in that relationship. Both you (individually) and your business (corporately) would regularly bring issues to God in prayer and seek his leading through the Scriptures as well as through the active involvement of the Holy

Spirit. The challenge of creating a sustainable business would engage the entire household, providing a group purpose, a topic of conversation, and an identity for the entire group. You would be adding a new dimension to family meetings, prayer, and Bible study time. Your focus would now be bigger and more "other-driven" than before.

You would seek out biblical teaching and teachers who could shed light on your challenges and provide you guidance on all the issues you would confront: financing, sales, operational systems, vendor relationships, marketing, human resources, etc. Instead of just going to church and expecting the pastor to feed you spiritually, you would have a pressing need to learn specifically what the Word could tell you about situations as they came up. You would become proactive and focused on you and your family's engagement in the Bible.

You would understand the uses of money and seek ways to bless those less blessed financially than you. The business would provide plenty of opportunities to discuss and to bless those recipients and causes to whom you were led.

Secondly, the business would be a family business. That means that every family member who was able would have a role in the business. The business would be a mechanism to teach work ethic, responsibility, relationships, ethics, etc., like none other. The growth of the business, both in economic terms as well as Christian influence, would be a top-of-the-mind expectation for the entire family.

The business would create an expectation and environment where children could gain a sense of something larger than themselves and a responsibility beyond themselves. The likelihood of them becoming involved in substance abuse, casual sex, and other maladies of the teenage years in this country would be dramatically decreased. Older family members would find a place to apply their wisdom and insights. Instead of whiling away in a facility, they would be expected to bring value to the organization.

As the head of the household, you would be challenged in a greater way to grow spiritually, make wise decisions for the good of every member, and lead the assemblage spiritually. Your more rapid spiritual growth would enlarge your perception of your responsibilities, and you would become a shepherd of your employees. You would begin by influencing them with your relationship with God and progress to pastoring them. You would see yourself as the pastor of your flock—the family members, employees, vendors, and customers who would interact with you.

Finally, it would be business, not a mission effort. The purpose would be first to create economic survival for the family and then prosperity for the household by providing valuable goods and services to your customers. Your business would focus on generating profits and then investing those profits in its own growth, in the individual members of the household, and in individuals and organizations that the Holy Spirit brought to your attention. Your business would be a means of taking back the physical creation for the Kingdom, in the front lines of the battle to establish Christ in every nook and cranny of this creation. You would think, not in terms of "Business as Mission," but rather that your business was a ministry --"Business is Ministry."

Impact on the larger economy

Now consider thousands of biblical businesses sprouting all over the country and proliferating across the globe. Specifically, what would happen if we could multiply the number of biblical businesses by a multiple of ten in the next ten years? What would be the impact?

In every industry, geography, and people group, the proliferation of Christian business would bring salt and light into the darkness. By setting standards of integrity, concern for human beings, and ethical conduct, Christian businesses would draw the attention of people from every sphere— politicians, investors, customers, vendors, and neighbors.

Christian businesses would establish themselves first in the area that is of primary concern to every human being— the physical world of food, clothing, and shelter. They would be a beacon for everyone that they touched. As those in their spheres of influence saw the spirituality that produced the organization and its practices, they would be attracted to the source: Jesus Christ.

The worldwide church would grow both in numbers, as the lifestyle became attractive to people, and in depth and maturity. New converts, instead of being left on their own, would have already been surrounded by role models, mentors, and leaders in the biblical businesses that employed them. They would grow in their faith as they interacted with those around them.

Economies would be stabilized and grown. Because the heads of households would be guided by the Scriptures, they would use debt far less than their non-Christian cohorts, thus buffering them from the more dramatic impacts of the up-and-down business cycle. They truly would be beacons of light in the darkness.

The culture would be impacted. Just as the gay rights movement—a mobilized small minority of people—was able to change the cultural perceptions in ten years or so, Christian businesses, a much larger group, could affect the cultural perceptions of Jesus

Christ and the Kingdom of God. Christianity would no longer be perceived to be about the institutional church; rather it would be about the reality of the Kingdom touching people where they lived.

Christ would gain influence. Christian businesses would affect people first economically through a job or transactions flavored with Christian ethics. Then they would affect the culture socially as their ethics and Christ-centeredness attracted people to their lifestyle. As the influence of these businesses expanded, the culture would be seasoned with the salt of the Kingdom. The passages commanding us to be salt and light in the world would take on a whole new level of meaning and significance.

Just as it did in the first generation following the resurrection, Christianity, expressing itself through businesses, would evidence itself as an alternative lifestyle. But in a world characterized by darkness and confusion, that alternative lifestyle would be attractive and would grow until it impacted the culture, bringing God's light to the world.

There is not a societal problem today that could not be significantly alleviated by the culture and lifestyle of the Christian business. It could be the solution to our most pressing economic and cultural problems.

There would be no room for substance abuse, for example, as it diminishes the employees ability to perform.

Children, who in today's Western culture are often seen as economic liabilities, have little responsibility to contribute to the family. They often arrive at adulthood with a little sense of purpose, a college degree, and massive student loan debt. In the household culture, they would be expected to contribute to the business, thereby gaining a sense of accomplishment, self-worth, identity, and purpose that will stand out. In the process, they will gain knowledge and skills that will serve them and the business well into the future.

Poverty and homelessness would be impacted by the generous giving and focused charity of the Spirit-lead household.

> The proliferation of Christian businesses— God's business primacy strategy -- is a significant part of God's plan for the restoration of a stable world-wide economy.

Thinking about this chapter...

1. Think about what it would like if you were to head or have a significant responsibility in a Christian business.

2. Which of the implications on the economy that were discussed in this chapter most resonate with you?

3. What other implications do you anticipate?

FOURTEEN

What Hinders Us?

When you consider all the positive benefits that come with biblical businesses and add that to the overwhelming weight of the scriptural evidence for them, some questions come to mind:

Why haven't we changed the world by proliferating biblical businesses?

Why is this concept—that a business can be a force for the Kingdom and was designed by God to be the primary thrust to redeem creation—so foreign to so many of us?

Why are there thousands of Christians in businesses who don't see themselves as involved with a spiritual entity? In this chapter, I'm going to suggest some answers.

First, lets establish three principles:

1. God doesn't see things the way we see them.
He said this through the prophet Isaiah:

> "For My thoughts are not your thoughts, nor are your ways My ways," declares the Lord. "For as the heavens are higher than the earth, so are My ways higher than your ways And My thoughts than your thoughts." (Isa. 55:8–9)

We see this principle played out in the Bible over and over again. One of the most poignant examples was the call by the Hebrews for a king. Here's the scenario: the Hebrews had settled in the promised land, and God had established a system of governance built around prophets and judges. With these two groups of people in regular relationship with God, there was no need for a human system of government. But the Hebrew people wanted to be like those around them, who were governed by kings. They clamored for a king. God finally relents and selects Saul as the first king. It wasn't his first choice. He tells the prophet, Samuel, "It is not you they have rejected as their king, it is me" (1 Sam. 8:7).

Some good, from a human perspective, came out of the institution of a system of kings. The Israelites defeated their enemies in battle, power was centralized around the king, and under Solomon, the Israelite state achieved great prosperity and influence.

However, in the big picture, the results were devastating. The Israeli people lost their reliance on prophets and judges and thus moved further away from God. Their focus often strayed from the things of God to worldly issues. Power struggles and moral corruption became commonplace. The kings led the nation into idolatry on numerous occasions. Most of the kings were corrupt. And the institution of the rule of kings led to the division into two kingdoms and eventually to the loss of the ten tribes.

They missed it. Instead of following the simple, direct system that God had created for them, the Israelite people built a worldly system of institutions and powerful people. That was their downfall. They missed God's plan for them and substituted a man- made institution in its place.

2. Our ideas, particularly our deep-seated, fundamental beliefs—often called paradigms—shape and dictate our behavior.

The classic example of this was the Middle Ages belief—deep-seated, universally accepted—that the world was flat. Since the world was flat, or so it was believed, there was no reason to attempt to sail around it. Millions of people were shackled by this belief, and the urge to explore the boundaries of creation was hindered by this false paradigm. It took Columbus and his epic journey to reveal the false paradigm.

While not so dramatic, we all have ideas and paradigms that influence and shape our behavior. Some of these are individual, while others are commonly held by communities of people. It is easier to point out the false paradigms in other cultures, people groups, and other individuals than it is to recognize them in ourselves. Our personal paradigms are so deeply held that they operate at the subconscious level, influencing our behavior and attitudes without us even being aware of them. So, it's entirely possible, even likely, that all of us have some false and damaging paradigms lurking in the deep recesses of our minds and souls and influencing our attitudes and behaviors in ways that are ultimately detrimental to our spiritual health, both individually and in the community.

> So, it's entirely possible, even likely, that almost all of us have some false and damaging paradigms lurking in the deep recesses of our minds and souls and influencing our attitudes and behaviors in ways that are ultimately detrimental to our spiritual health, both individually and in the community.

3. An image of how we hinder the Holy Spirit.

Some years ago, I was given this image of how our ideas and paradigms can hinder our understanding of God's plans for us.

Imagine a bright and powerful light in the form of a

globe. That is like the power of the Holy Spirit within us, enlightening our understanding, doing away with our false paradigms, and operating powerfully within our life. Now build the framework of a box around the globe so that each of the sides is framed with an outline of a rectangle. That framework is like our physical bodies within which the globe—the Holy Spirit— resides.

Now take a screen, like the kind you put on windows to keep the bugs out. And nail it over one side of that framework. You'll note that the screen slightly hinders the light. It still shines, but not quite as brightly. Now, nail multiple screens, one on top of the other, over all the exposed sides of the framework, until the light within cannot penetrate the multiple layers of screens, and it becomes dark. Those multiple screens are the false paradigms that we gradually acquire that serve to hinder the power of the Holy Spirit in our lives. No one of them is powerful enough to shut off the light, but when a number are applied over and over, the sum total keeps the light boxed in.

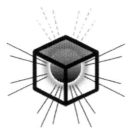

Now back to our questions.

Why haven't we changed the world by proliferating biblical businesses?

Why is this concept—that a business can be a force for the Kingdom and in fact was designed by God to be the primary thrust to redeem creation—so foreign to so many of us?

Why are there thousands of Christians in businesses who don't see themselves as involved with a spiritual entity?

The answer is this. We have allowed some false paradigms to shut out the truth of the biblical teaching on businesses as we've chosen to follow man-made ideas rather than the powerful truth the Bible teaches. We've assembled a whole host of errant, man-made ideas that have boxed in the power of the biblical teaching.

> We haven't seen the biblical teaching on businesses because we have not looked for it. We haven't looked for it because we've been content to allow false ideas to direct our attitudes and our behaviors.

The list of paradigms and ideas that hinder us stretches for quite a way. It's beyond the scope of this book to list them all. Instead, I'm going to focus on only two. One comes from our popular culture, and the other comes from the institutional church culture. Let's look at some of the ideas that hinder the power of biblical businesses in our culture.

From our popular culture, we find the first false Idea: Business is just about making money.

The most deceptive ideas always contain a grain of the truth. This one does too. Business is about making money. But it is not *just* about making money.

From a worldly perspective, businesses are formed to provide for the economic security of the folks who own and work in that business. Since food and shelter are basic needs, a business, to be viable, must meet those needs. And it does that by providing goods and services for money. Money then becomes one of the keys to any business. A business that doesn't create sufficient income is not going to stay in business for long.

The problem arises when the business people focus solely on money as the rationale for the business. When they do that, they miss all the other incredible benefits that accrue to themselves, their employees, their families, their customers, and to society in general.

A business doesn't necessarily have to create profits, but it does need to be sustainable. In other words, money is important. It's a core reason for starting a business. But profits aren't nearly as important as sustainability. And profits aren't just for the purpose of buying the business owner a better car or bigger home. As we saw in the parable of the bags of gold, reinvesting in the growth of the business is a biblical strategy. Profits fund and empower growth.

Unfortunately, our popular culture promotes a distorted picture of the purpose of a business. The media glorify the "self-made" millionaire, Wall Street awards huge bonuses for those who reach revenue goals, and CEOs are awarded obscene bonuses for achieving quarterly results in publicly held companies. The emphasis on making money has never been more pronounced or glorified.

It is thus really easy for the business person to react to the popular culture and define the success of the business solely in monetary terms. When we believe the idea that business is just about money, we never see the powerful entity for good that a biblical business could be because we never look for it. We need to take this idea—that business is just about money—pry it off, and discard it in the trash.

From the institutional church culture, we find the second false idea:

God's work—real ministry—is only done under the auspices of established religion, that which I call the institutional church system.

This message is proclaimed verbally and more powerfully and is implicit on so many levels that it is almost impossible to be a churchgoer and not absorb this idea. Church buildings are often referred to as

"God's house;" pastors are often imbued with some special authority, and giving to the local church is held up as a prerequisite for the Christian life. All these together combine to send the message that "real ministry" is only done under the auspices of the established institution.

The problem with it is twofold: first, it is not biblical, and second, the impact of believing it is devastating.

Lets look at the biblical position on God's work.

> Whatever you do, work at it with all your heart, as working for the Lord, not for men, since you know that you will receive an inheritance from the Lord as a reward. It is the Lord Christ you are serving. (Col. 3:23–24)

The Scriptures teach that no work is better, more blessed, or more holy than any other. Whatever you do, whether it is under the auspices of organized religion or not, is important because of for whom you do it, not what you do.

Whenever we create a word to describe something, like "ministry," by that simple act, we imply the existence of things that are not that thing. For example, if we say that we are "Americans," that statement implies that there are other folks who are "non-Americans." When we hear pastors proclaim that the church building is "God's house," that implies that everything else is not.

And therein lies the problem. When we hold some work apart as being a ministry, we are in effect saying that all other work is not ministry. When we say that "ministry work" is special, we are, at the same time, saying that all other work is ordinary and not special.

> When we say that true ministry is only done within the auspices of the organized church, we say that it can't be done outside of it. And when we do that, we remove God and his power from all work that doesn't fit established religion's definition of ministry.

For a Christian, there is no such thing as work that is "non-ministry"—except that which is sin. Everything done in service to our Lord—every thought we think, every breath we take, every action we make—is either service to the Lord or sin.

The practical effects of believing this paradigm have been devastating. Unfortunately, countless millions of people have lived lives that have been narrowed and hemmed in by this false idea. There are thousands of Christian businesspeople who hold to this false concept of ministry. Since some things are "ministry" and some are not, so the thinking goes, then their businesses are "not ministry" and are relegated to the world of the ordinary, nonspecial "everything else."

These Christian brothers and sisters are, therefore, hindered from seeing their businesses as powerful, holy entities in the forefront of the Kingdom's advance into every nook forefront of the Kingdom's advance into every nook and cranny of the economy. Millions of people have not looked for God in their work. The idea that

God instituted work as the first place where he would interact with them remains hidden to millions. We haven't seen that truth because we haven't looked for it. We haven't looked for it because we've believed errant ideas.

The net impact of this paradigm has been devastating to the Christian faith. According to researcher George Barna, the institutional church system has spent $530 billion dollars on itself in the past couple of decades and has not increased the percentage of Christians by even one percent.[6]

What an incredible waste of gifts, talents, time, and energy! Satan must love this idea. Look at all the power of the Holy Spirit he has hindered and kept contained over multiple nations and many generations. It must be one of his favorites.

> We haven't seen the truth about biblical businesses because we haven't looked for it. We haven't looked for it because we have been content to believe errant ideas.

These are just two of the ideas that have served to box in the light of the Holy Spirit's teachings about biblical businesses. There are dozens of others. The focus of this book prevents us from creating an exhaustive list. One place to look, if you are interested in digging deeper, is my companion book, *Is the Institutional Church Really the Church?*[7] which is described in the back pages of this manuscript. Or visit my blog posts at

davekahle.com/wordpressblogs/category/kingdom-issues.

The reason we haven't seen that light is that we have not looked for it. The ideas rampant in our culture have us focused elsewhere. If biblical businesses are going to regain their rightful place in the Kingdom, these errant ideas must be pried off the box and thrown into the trash bin of history, to join "the world is flat" and all the other false paradigms that have hindered the Kingdom's cause.

Biblical incidents of professional, located "pastors" leading churches in the New Testament = 0

Incidents of business leaders leading their employees to accept Christ = 4

Incidents of churches meeting in dedicated church buildings = 0

Incidents of churches meeting in the homes of business leaders = 5

Thinking about this chapter...

1. To what degree is it possible that we see things—particularly the role of business—differently than God does?

2. To what degree do you agree with this statement: "So it's entirely possible, even likely, that almost all of

us have some false and damaging paradigms lurking in the deep recesses of our minds and souls and influencing our attitudes and behaviors in ways that are ultimately detrimental to our spiritual health, both individually and that of our communities."

3. To what extent is it possible that some of our deep- seated ideas actually hinder the workings of the Holy Spirit in our lives and our communities?

4. To what extent do you agree with this statement: "We haven't seen the biblical teaching on businesses because we have not looked for it. We haven't looked for it because we've been content to allow false ideas to direct our attitudes and our behaviors."

5. To what degree do you agree or disagree with the idea that "true ministry is only done within the auspices of the institutional church?"

Biblical Business Profile: The Innogroup Companies

Mike Lanser, CEO of Innotech, credits the owners of the Prince Corporation to planting the idea in him that a company could have a purpose larger than just making money. The family that originally formed the Prince Corporation saw the business as a means of generating income that they could then give away to fund charitable works.

He and his brother, Brian, were engineers at the Prince Corporation when they saw an opportunity to outsource some of the manufacturing processes to a company that they would start. Prince gave them a contract, and in 1992, Innotech began with Mike, Brian, and their father at the helm.

Before starting the business, each wrote a one-page document detailing their ideas as to what a business could be and why they wanted to form this business. Out of that came a consensus that the business should be built on biblical principles. What exactly that meant is an understanding that has evolved. Originally, the concept was just to use some of the company's profits for charitable causes. To this day, a fixed percentage of the company's profits are donated. As the company evolved and grew, so did its view as to what constituted a biblicallybasedcompany.

Their unique employee benefits grew out of that conviction. For example, every employee gets three weeks' vacation and can take an additional two weeks if they donate that time to a charitable cause. Every seven years, every employee may take a three-month sabbatical devoted to personal development.

As their understanding of what it means to become a biblical business evolved, it eventually became codified in their 'Fourteen Dimensions" statement.

Fourteen Dimensions
1. Culture of Character ["being"]
2. Wellness [physical, emotional, relational]
3. Giving Time
4. Giving Talent
5. Giving Money
6. Growing Spiritually
7. Earth-keeping
8. Loving and caring for others
9. Providing jobs
10. Growing people [impact and ability]
11. Where we chose to do business [BLB vs. LLB]
12. Choice of products and services [visors, orphans, bullets, design...]
13. Investing ourreputation

14. Sharing what we have learned
- Inside > Great Operations
- External > Impact

In a backyard discussion among the three principals of "how do we play big and still feel small?" Brian came up with the concept that was to multiply the company's impact—to create a matrix of compatible companies, all connected in some way to Innotech but with independent management.

With that concept, the first company, Ventura Manufacturing, was started in 1997 to take on some manufacturing processes that were not in the heart of Innotech's strengths. That first company established the pattern that was repeated a dozen times. Innotech would provide the business seed and a degree of supervision while retaining a minority ownership in the new business. Today, the eclectic group of for-profit and nonprofit enterprises includes Inno-Versity, InnoGroup Foundation, iCademy Global, Innocademy, Vortec Tooling, Ventura Manufacturing, Inontime, and Venture Source. As a group, they estimate they employ around one thousand people and do a couple of hundred million dollars of annual sales.

Not that their growth has been uneventful. The recession of 2008 was brutal for the companies. As Mike tells it, the company had invested heavily in three areas of growth. They were not fully developed when the recession hit. The banks refused to lend, and the company's cash flow was severely restricted. The company got behind with its vendors, and the bank put them in a workout program. "It costs us about $2 million in extra fees when we could least afford it," Mike said. There was no choice but to double down and bring the three efforts to fruition by hard work. And they did, but at a big cost of stress and energy. "The aftereffects are still being felt around here,' Mike reflected.

One of the issues that are on the top of Mike's list these days is business succession. While the company is 25 percent ESOP-owned, the questions of how to pass on the principles and values to another generation and provide for an eventual leadership transition occupy a large portion of his time.

As they look ahead, the companies continue to refine what it means to be a biblical business and together pursue a vision of creating "128 points of light that help 10,000 people impact peoples lives.'

FIFTEEN

What to Do Now? An Action Plan for a Way Forward

═══════════════════════════════════════

I have made the case that the reason we have not discovered the biblical teaching on businesses is that no one was looking. And the reason why no one was looking has to do with the false paradigms that have occupied our belief system.

If we are going to create a world where biblical businesses regain their rightful place in the Kingdom, then we must change the paradigms that are routinely accepted in modern Christianity.

Within five years, we could change the culture's paradigms, discarding those that hinder and replacing them with affirming ideas that support the proliferation of biblical businesses. Within ten years, we could multiply the number of biblical businesses operating in the world by a factor of ten (at least). In so doing, we could extend the Kingdom into every nook and cranny of our culture and economy. In a decade, we can change the world.

We know it is possible. We have a model in the gay rights movement. Within a decade, the entire nation's ideas on gay rights and gay marriage were transformed. Three percent of the population changed the thinking of the majority of the population. Now we can use the same strategies to penetrate the world with the Kingdom.

Lets get into the details of how that would work.

The Wikipedia encyclopedia accurately articulates the necessities for changing a paradigm:

> Another use of the word *paradigm* is in the sense of "worldview." For example, in social science, the term is used to describe the set of experiences, beliefs, and values that affect the way an individual perceives reality and responds to that perception. Social scientists have adopted the Kuhnian phrase "paradigm shift" to denote a change in how a given society goes about organizing and understanding reality. A "dominant paradigm" refers to the values, or system of thought, in a society that are most standard and widely held at a given time. Dominant paradigms are shaped both by the community's cultural background and by the context of the historical moment. The following are conditions that facilitate a system of thought to become an accepted dominant paradigm:
>
> - Professional organizations that give legitimacy to the paradigm
>
> - Dynamic leaders who introduce and purport the paradigm

- Journals and editors who write about the system of thought. They both disseminate the information essential to the paradigm and give the paradigm legitimacy

- Government agencies who give credence to the paradigm

- Educators who propagate the paradigm's ideas by teaching it to students

- Conferences conducted that are devoted to discussing ideas central to the paradigm

- Media coverage

- Lay groups, or groups based around the concerns of lay persons, that embrace the beliefs central to the paradigm

- Sources of funding to further research on the paradigm[9]

Let's use this bit of research as a pattern to go forward. Here's how each one of the bullet points listed above could be brought to bear on the task of changing our paradigms. If we are going to change the world by utilizing God's primary phalanx into a lost and hurting world, we need...

Professional organizations that give legitimacy to the paradigm.

There is a national association for almost every trade group, profession, and industry. Suppose Biblical business owners could lobby those associations to create subgroups of Biblical businesses. We could, within a couple of years, have hundreds or even thousands of professional organizations within the existing framework of biblical businesses devoted to promulgating the pattern.

Dynamic leaders who introduce and support the paradigm

People who already have positions of influence via their writing or speaking could begin to present the idea of a biblical business within the context of their current message. There are thousands of business leaders, bloggers, authors, and consultants who could work this concept into their messages, using existing spheres of influence to proclaim the message. This could begin within months.

Pastors particularly could use their pulpits and influence to promote a more biblical view of the Kingdom and hold up the primacy of biblical businesses as God's first choice to carry the Kingdom of economic security, spiritual development, and spiritual gifts into every nook and cranny of the culture. They could begin this next week.

Journals and editors who write about the system of thought. They both disseminate the information essential to the paradigm and give the paradigm legitimacy.

Once again, all that is necessary is for the folks who currently occupy these positions to begin to publicize the idea, give exposure to biblical business events, and proactively cover the emerging movement. Within a couple of years, hundreds of journals, editors, and journalists could be contributing to the movement.

Government agencies who give credence to the paradigm

Imagine employees and managers in hundreds of government agencies—federal, state, county, and city—deciding to interpret their mandates in such a way as to promote faith-based business initiatives. It could certainly be done. We saw that same principle in operation when the Obama IRS chose to delay applications for nonprofit status from conservative organizations. Suppose some of those same bureaucrats decided to do exactly the opposite—to use their influence to support and promote faith- based businesses. It has been done. It can be done.

At the same time, legislatures at every level— federal, state, county, city—could craft legislation to support and promote the efforts of biblical businesses. We saw this same strategy enacted by the gay rights movement. What started as a number of vocal spokespeople eventually morphed into legislation favorable to their cause at every level of government. So we know the strategy works. Now let's turn it to Kingdom advantage.

Educators who propagate the paradigm's ideas by teaching it to students.

Suppose professors and administrators at Christian colleges accepted the challenge to change the paradigms of their students and began to teach and prepare their students for the higher calling of running a biblical business. Within five years, thousands of students could be graduated who were prepared and empowered to contribute to the movement. They could really "prepare the saints for works of service."

Educators in nonreligious institutions could do the same. We see courses developed for various aspects of gay rights, women's rights, etc. Now, courageous college and high school educators could create courses and modules within existing courses to give visibility and credibility to the biblical business rights movement.

Conferences conducted that are devoted to discussing ideas central to the paradigm.

Conference planners of all sorts—influential individuals, associations, bloggers, etc.— could organize conferences all over the world to expose people to the concept of a biblical business and release them from the paradigms that have kept them bottled up. Separate tracks that focus on biblical businesses could be added to existing events almost immediately.

We have already seen some these conferences occur. These existing conferences just need to focus on tearing off the screens that hinder our thinking, doing away with the ideas and paradigms that have hindered us, and replacing them with Kingdom-affirming, biblical-business-promoting paradigms.

Media coverage.

Folks in the media could choose to spotlight events, people, and circumstances that shed light on the movement. This growing media coverage would add credibility and visibility to the movement. Again, we know it can be done because it already has been done. The gay rights movement is an example. In a matter of a decade, almost the entire nation changed its beliefs about gay marriage. Media coverage that was inclined to publicize and promote the movement was in large measure responsible. We can use that same strategy to promote the Kingdom-building, life- affirming message of biblical businesses.

Lay groups, or groups based on the concerns of lay persons, that embrace the beliefs central to the paradigm.

The writer of this list obviously operates from the paradigm that there are clergy and lay people, and the two are separate and distinct groups. We deny this idea. There is no biblical basis for this idea, and the concept is one of those ideas that hold people hostage and nail screens on the power of the Spirit within their lives. There are no clergy, and there are no lay people;

there are only Christians.

The fact that this item appears on this list only goes to illustrate how universally accepted and deeply held are the false paradigms that hinder the movement.

Sources of funding to further research on the paradigm.

Existing funds could simply add criteria to their guidelines that identify and value businesses that are striving to fit the biblical business mold. Angel investors could do the same. Companies looking to make acquisitions could add criteria to their list of characteristics they seek to identify and more highly value candidates who are striving to become biblical businesses.

With just a slight change in perspective, millions, if not billions, of dollars of investment funds could be released to promote Kingdom businesses. This could be done within months.

Small groups of biblical business people could form investment and mentoring groups and seek to birth, promote, and nurture biblical businesses in their sphere of influence.

The strategy is proven. The infrastructure is in existence. The people necessary to make it happen are already in place. We could really and truly change the paradigms that have hindered us in five years. In ten years, we can multiply the number of biblical businesses worldwide by a factor of ten, at least. In ten years, we can penetrate every nook and cranny in the world economy and season it with the salt of biblical businesses. We can change the world in ten years. All that is necessary are courageous, Spirit-led individuals willing to take up the message, roll up their sleeves, and get into the business of multiplying the number of biblical businesses.

If you occupy one of the positions mentioned in the list above, then you have the opportunity to have a significant impact by using your position to proactively promote the ideas we have unveiled.

If you are a young person considering an education and a career...

Carefully consider the ministry of heading or being a part of a Christian business. It will provide you with a lifetime of challenge and an opportunity to live out the one-anothers in daily interactions with employees, family members, customers, suppliers, and other stockholders. You will be in the forefront of God's phalanx to take back creation. You will have an opportunity to multiply your influence, provide for the poor, and increase your family's wealth. The world and God's kingdom need you.

If a business isn't in your scope, consider one of the professions and roles listed above. You can use the influence and position you gain to push forward the biblical business agenda.

If you are a pastor...

If you have been guilty of promoting the errant ideas that have served to hinder the release of biblical businesses in your congregation, it's time to change your focus.

Then consider using your influence to encourage the growth of the kingdom, not just the attendance at your church. Understand that it is in the household—the Christian business—where real discipleship takes place and where people are converted, ministered to, and held accountable. Begin to think of your church as a place where heads of households can be equipped, supported, and encouraged—a place to serve the businesses and the businesspeople that God has chosen to be the phalanx of his Kingdom.

A solution for local congregations

Suppose you, the pastor, began to understand that the biblical business is God's first choice for penetrating the world with the Kingdom, of providing economic security for people, and for interacting with him. What could you do?

Heres one specific initiative:

1. Encourage the businesspeople in your congregation to see their businesses as God's first choice to penetrate the world with the Kingdom.

2. Encourage the development of business skills among the congregation.

3. Create a "business development team" among your congregants, with the specific charge to nurture the inception and growth of biblical businesses within the congregation.

4. Direct a large percentage of your revenue to a fund directed by the business development team that would help fund the beginning and the expansion of biblical businesses.

5. Encourage and equip their congregants to see their businesses as "mini-congregations" and encourage their business owner to accept the responsibility to "pastor' their employees.

If you are an administrator at a Christian college...

If you have been guilty of promoting the errant ideas that have served to hinder the release of biblical businesses in your college, it's time to change your focus.

Then understand that producing hundreds of Christian entrepreneurs, equipped and encouraged to create Christian businesses around the world, is a higher calling than producing pastors. Turn your seminaries into training grounds of young Christian entrepreneurs. Train the next generation of heads of households to occupy the ground that has been dismissed and ignored for generations. Take the lead in restoring the biblical business to its rightful place in the kingdom of God. Develop this understanding in all the students in your institution. Fill the spaces noted in the bullet list of paradigm- changing initiatives with graduates who are energized to change the world through biblical businesses.

If you are currently a Christian businessperson...

Give thanks for the special ministry the Lord has given to you. If you are employed in a non-Christian company, learn all you can and be a reliable, profitable employee. Understand that you are where you are for a reason. Pray that the Lord would show you whether He wants you to become a Christian entrepreneur. Ask that he open those doors, if that is what he has for you.

Consider the Biblical Business Course[10] as a way to understand how to shape your business into the biblical business mold.

If you are an owner of a Christian business...

Give thanks for the special ministry the Lord has given you. Begin to see your business as the vanguard of the Lord's army—charged with growing wealth and influence and providing a mechanism for providing employment, a Christian work environment, a place where the one-anothers can be implemented on a daily basis. Your organization is the nucleus for the church, the vanguard in the Lord's efforts to convert the world and establish the Kingdom in every nook and cranny of this world.

Consider the Biblical Business Course[10] as a first step toward understanding how to mold your business into a biblical business.

If you are a worker or an employee and do not see yourself as having the resources or interest in starting your own business...

Give thanks for the special ministry the Lord has given you. You are the subject of several of Jesus's parables. Consider your role a sacred one. If you work for a non-Christian enterprise, consider yourself to be the salt and light in that organization. Ask the Lord to strengthen your witness and empower you to practice the one-anothers with all those around you. Strive to be a profitable and reliable employee and a trusted coworker. If you work in a Christian family business, give thanks for the special ministry the Lord has given you. You provide the operational wisdom and insight that powers the Christian family business. Your job is bigger than just your job. You are a part of the Lord's army, building wealth, gaining influence, and extending the Lord's providence to those around you and to everyone that your organization touches.

If you are a professional who serves biblical businesses...

Understand that few Christian-owned businesses see themselves as biblical businesses, in the forefront of God's phalanx to take back the creation and proliferate the Kingdom. The paradigms of the institutional church system have them thinking far less of themselves and their businesses.

Work to educate them and free them from the shackle of the negative paradigms that have functioned to keep their businesses contained within

> The infrastructure is already in place. The strategy is proven. All we need are courageous individuals ready to take on the established ideas and promote biblical businesses. You may be one of them. Now is the time.

the ranks of the spiritually impotent. Help them to see themselves as powerful knights in God's army and their businesses as the front line in the battle. The infrastructure is already in place. The strategy is proven. All we need are courageous individuals ready to take on the established ideas and promote biblical businesses. You may be one of them. Now is the time.

SIXTEEN

Final Thoughts

━━━━━━━━━━━━━━━━━━━━━━━━━━━━━━━━━━━

We've **blown it.** We had the greatest nation in the history of the world, with a culture that celebrated Christianity and reflected those values. In a couple of generations, we have lost that culture, lost those values, and put a halt to the increase in Christians. We now have a culture that celebrates decadent values and in which the percentage of evangelical Christians is decreasing annually.

We have blown it because we have missed it. We missed the clear teaching in the Bible—from the beginning in Genesis to the end of the New Testament—that clearly portrays the household (biblical businesses) as God's priority in the battle to redeem creation and all its people. We've missed it because we have believed the false and dangerous paradigms of conventional wisdom—

from the popular culture that business is just about money and from the religious establishment that real ministry is only done within the programs of the church, making business a second-class endeavor.

We've believed those paradigms, and that belief has led to an unprecedented hindering of the power of the Holy Spirit to impact people and culture—millions of businesspeople thinking of themselves as second-class Christians, millions of people who could have been led to Christ, and were not, millions of people existing in poverty when they could have been lifted out of it by growing biblical businesses.

However, we do not have to be deceived anymore. We, Kingdom businesspeople, have to accept the responsibility to bring business back to its rightful place in the Kingdom and to unleash its power to create jobs, touch people, develop them spiritually, encounter God, and penetrate the darkness with light.

In the first chapter, I wrote this:

> I am not naive enough to believe that this book alone is going to convince multitudes of people to change some of the paradigms that have been drilled into them by the institutional church and the culture.

> But I believe I have a responsibility to start the conversation. While the resistance to what I have to say may be extraordinary, my hope is that my saying it will release others to push forward. God has created a movement. We can jump into it and have a role in changing the world.

You may not agree with everything I have written. That's okay. The point is this: the movement has begun. There are lots of places for individuals and organizations of all sorts to jump in, join God's work, and have a role in the next great movement of the Almighty in our lives.

You do not need to agree with me 100 percent to get a glimpse of what could be if we were to proliferate biblical businesses. Join the movement.

Get involved. Find your place. In five years, we can change the commonly accepted errant paradigms. In ten years, we can multiply the number of biblical businesses in the world by a factor of ten. We can change the world. Lets do it.

> In five years, we can change the commonly accepted errant paradigms. In ten years, we can multiply the number of biblical businesses in the world by a factor of ten. We can change the world. Lets do it.

Dave Kahle is available to speak with your group or help your business grow. Visit The Biblical Business Course and take a class to begin your growth. Visit:

www.thebiblicalbusiness.com

Notes

1. Neighmond, Patti. "People Who Feel They Have a Purpose in Life Live Longer." www.npr.org/sections/health-shots/2014/07/28/334447274/people- who-feel-they-have-a-purpose-in-life-live-longer

2. The Council of Economic Advisors. "Nine Facts about American Families and Work. https://www.whitehouse.gov/sites/default/files/docs/nine_facts_aboutfamily_and_work_real_final.pdf

3. The Alternative Board. "New Survey Shows Work-Life Balance is Possible, But Not Likely for Entrepreneurs." www.thealternativeboard.com/new-survey-shows-work-life-balance-is-possible-but-not-likely-for-entrepreneurs

4. Bosker, Bianca. 'Sheryl Sandberg: Theres No Such Thing as Work-Life Balance.' *The Huffington Post.* www.huffingtonpost.com/2012/04/06/sheryl-sandbergn_1409061.html

5. Collins, Ken. "Cultural Differences: Household," http://kencollins.com/explanations/why-10.htm

6. Barna, George, as quoted by Hillman, Os, *Faith&Work,* an e-book by Os Hillman, p. 31, Marketplace Leaders.

7. Kahle, Dave. *Is the Institutional Church Really the Church?* Tate Publications, 2014.

8. Kahle, Dave. "Cataract beliefs #2: I am required to give my tithe to the local church." http://bit.ly/2kuV9JD

9. *Wikipedia.*"Concept of paradigm and the social sciences, Paradigm." https://en.wikipedia.org/wiki/Paradigm.

10. The Biblical Business Course is a set of lessons by Dave Kahle, designed to help businesspeople take steps to turn their business into the biblical pattern. To review it, visit: https://bit.ly/2MxatTX.

Other Books by Dave Kahle

All books are available from the websites listed, or wherever business books are sold.

Is the Institutional Church Really the Church?

In the last 20 years, the institutional church has spent $530 Billion on itself, and not increased the percentage of Christians in this country by even one percent. Isn't it time someone asked some questions? Dave Kahle does. This book will change your views of the church forever. http://www.davekahle.com/wordpressblogs/institutional -church-really-church/

How to Sell Anything to Anyone Anytime

This book is in a class by itself. It has been:
- Named one of the Top Five Business Books by getAbstract in the April, 2011 edition of *Next*, the customermagazine by Price Water-houseCoopers.
- Named one of the Top Five Business Books by
- Handelsblatt, the biggest German-language
- business and finance newspaper.
- Named one of the top Ten English Business books in Austria by WirtschaftsBlatt, Austria's only business daily.
- Translated into Malaysian English, and available in Malaysia.
- Translated into both Complex and Simplified Chinese, and available throughout China.
- Translated into Latin American Spanish, and available throughout Latin America.
- Available in Malaysian English in Malaysia and Singapore.

- Available in a Kindle edition in Germany.
- Available as a Kindle edition in Italy.
- Available as a Kindle edition in the U. K.

If you want to grow your business, this is the book to read. http://www.davekahle.com/wordpressblogs/sell-anything-anyone-anytime/

The Heart of a Christian Salesperson

'Being a Christian sales person is going to be tricky.'

That's what I thought as I entered my first professional sales position. In retrospect, my life as a Christian sales person was confusing, gut-wrenchingly difficult, frustrating and wonderfully rewarding. I dealt with questions that you may also face:

- How do I balance the need to get results with the Christian ethic of leaving the outcomes to Christ?
- Where do I go for support and encouragement in a church where I'm seen as a second class citizen?
- How and when do I voice my beliefs on the job, when my employer is not paying me to do that?
- How do I maintain my perspective when some of the professional Christians around me are so much more. manipulative and deceitful than any secular acquaintance?
- How do I maintain my Christian ethics inside a company that supports just the opposite?
- How do I grow a consulting practice with no
- resources and no network?

Here's my story.
www.davekahle.com/wordpressblogs/heart-christian-sales-pereson

For other books by the author, visit www.davekahle.com

Final Thoughts

Take the next step in transforming your business into a biblical business!

Consider Dave Kahle's Biblical Business Course.

- A series of lessons designed to guide you through the first steps to turning your business into a biblical business. Learn more here: https://www.thebiblicalbusiness.com/biblical-business-coalition/
- For more resources to help you build a biblical business, visit: www.thebiblicalbusiness.com
- Sign up to receive regular postings here: https://www.davekahle.com/wordpressblogs/subscribe-daves-e-zines/
- Dave Kahle is available to speak with your group or help your business grow. Visit www.davekahle.com

If you think this is a message others should hear, will you...

Go to www.thegoodbookonbusiness.com and buy ten for $79 and give them to your friends and acquaintances.

And/or, go to the same website, and download a free facilitator's guide, which will allow you to facilitate 12 small group discussions on the book.

And/or, post a review on The Good Book on Business page on Amazon: www.amazon.com/Dave-Kahle/e/B001JS3SVK/